Beyond the Designation

What They Don't Teach You in RPA and CPM Classes

What I Have Learned and Experienced Over 29 Years in the Commercial Property Management Business

A Combination of Humorous Recollections from my 29 years in Commercial Property Management with some Life Lessons Learned and Useful Tips on Becoming the Best Professional Version of Oneself

Douglas W. Brewer, RPA, CPM, CCIM

Copyright © Douglas W. Brewer 2024

All Rights Reserved

No part of this publication may be reproduced, distributed, or transmitted in any form or by any means, including photocopying, recording, or other electronic or mechanical methods, without the author's prior written permission, except in the case of brief quotations embodied in critical reviews and certain other non-commercial uses permitted by copyright law. For permission requests, please get in touch with the author.

Contents

Dedication i
Acknowledgment iii
Foreword iv
Preface 1
Career Chronology and Markets Where I Had Asset Oversight; Designations and Awards 3
Chapter 1 "I Don't Know the Difference Between a Chiller and a Volkswagen Bus" 7
Chapter 2 "The Building Doesn't Have Enough Plumbing for Medical Use" 9
Chapter 3 "Do What You Say You are Going to Do" 12
Chapter 4 The Definition of Management 14
Chapter 5 "After 10 Years, She's a F**king Florist!" 16
Chapter 6 "That's One Way to Solve a Problem" 19
Chapter 7 Mentorship 22
Chapter 8 "Because You Get S**t Done" 28
Chapter 9 "You Are Already Wet" 30
Chapter 10 Bet on Yourself 33
Chapter 11 The Single Worst Decision Witnessed in My Property Management Career 41
Chapter 12 Core Beliefs of Highly Successful Property Management Teams .. 43
Chapter 13 Firing Someone 49
Chapter 14 Interesting Responses to Job Postings and Random Funny Lines ... 57
Chapter 15 Management and Leadership Principles I Have Come to Live By, or You Can't Make This S**t Up! 59
Chapter 16 Interviewing 69
Chapter 17 Email Writing Tips 72
Chapter 18 Leverage in Negotiating 74
Chapter 19 Some of My Favorite Quotes 78
Chapter 20 Heroin to Hand Grenades or My Travels Through Yeehaw Junction 83
Chapter 21 Evaluating Proposals and Getting the Best Bang for Your Buck 87
Chapter 22 Certificates of Insurance 91
Chapter 23 Year-End Annual Written Reviews 97
Chapter 24 My 15 Minutes of Fame 100
Chapter 25 Designations 106
Chapter 26 Promotions 108

Dedication

This Book and my career would not have been possible without the following individuals being who they were/are.

Gary Welch – Gary was a senior vice president with The Wilson Company in Tampa, FL. He hired me to manage perhaps the nicest Class A building in Tampa, located near the airport, Bayport Plaza. I had absolutely no real estate experience when he hired me, and, at the time, there were only two people on the planet who thought that was a good idea – him and me. Thank you for taking a (big) chance on me, Gary. May you rest in peace.

Bill P. Nikolis – I met Bill when he was an asset manager for Allegis, the real estate arm, at the time, of Aetna Life Insurance Company, the owner of Bayport Plaza. With both of us being from New York, we hit it off immediately. When Bill became the CEO of Delma Properties in New York, he took a chance on me by offering me a position as an asset manager when I only had property management experience. He liked to say he gave me enough rope to hang myself, but the flip side of that was that he allowed me the freedom to take chances and succeed. We have lost contact over the years, and I don't know if he is dead or alive, but he is one of my all-time favorite people. He used to say that I had the one attribute he valued above all others – loyalty.

Mukang Cho – Mook is the founder and CEO of Morning Calm Management in Boca Raton, FL. I worked for him for almost 13 years, and in my final self-assessment, I noted some of the things I learned about myself while doing so. I didn't know I could work 12 hours per day, 6+ days per week and look forward to going into the office the next day like it was Christmas. I didn't know I could genuinely care about the people in my property management and construction departments as much as I did about my own family. It took a while, but I didn't know that I could come to work with the overriding goal of making the people I work closely with a better version of their professional selves, with no regard for my own career advancement.

Acknowledgment

I would like to acknowledge the following individuals who have been instrumental in shaping my career.

Larry Finch

Sandra McBride

Barry Hanerfeld

Hank Brenner

Lis Wigmore

Bruce Wibbles

Colleen Maguire

Sandy Chase

Dan Levitan

Hilary Becker

Nina Gang

Scott Gray

Foreword

My name is Michele Micciche Dimond, RPA, CPM, CCIM, and I am Assistant Vice President of Operations for Schnitzer Properties' downtown office portfolio in Portland, Oregon. I met Doug Brewer in 2002 when I was working in St. Petersburg, Florida for Delma Properties. I had been given a lucky break to transition from the hospitality business to commercial property management. When I was hired, I admittedly knew nothing about commercial real estate, but they needed someone who was responsible, a fast learner and most of all, inexpensive, to manage a class A, 16-story, 243,000SF high rise with 22 office tenants and a 60-tenant executive suite operation. After a year, Doug was brought in to replace the person who had hired me and who had taught me "basic training-Real Estate 101". I instantly liked Doug. He was honest and frank, smart and capable, but what would he think of me? I had already survived for over a year in a sink or swim environment, but I was well aware that I had very limited property management experience. Working for Doug was like being in the military. Get up early to do inspections, be on time, have everything ship-shape with happy tenants. I noticed that Doug was observing everything I did, including how much time I spent in my office, and he was asking me a lot of probing, detailed questions. I worked hard to put my best foot forward, but would it be enough? Then, it came… the come-to-Jesus moment that I was suspecting, anticipating. I was called in for a meeting in his office. I needed the job. I needed this lucky break to continue. I wanted a career in the crazy and ever-changing world of commercial real estate. In 2002, it was still basically a man's business world, but here was a career where I had noticed that, in the Tampa Bay area, women dominated at the Property Manager level and were also in many senior positions. It was not a surprise that Doug told me that he needed me to be better. I told him, in phrasing I can no longer recall, that I was ready and willing to learn. Would he teach me? Would he be my mentor? Yes, he would. Thank God. Another blessing, another lucky break. I'm so glad that he has written this book. These tips and principles have guided me to a successful, rewarding, and enjoyable career for which I am very grateful. Whether you are just starting out in property management, considering it as a career opportunity or qualify as a seasoned veteran, you can benefit from this book. It's a fast and enjoyable read, filled with helpful information and a splash of dry Long Island wit. Enjoy!

Preface

I remember reading Mark McCormack's most influential book, What They Don't Teach You at Harvard Business School in the late 1980s and, besides it being a terrific read, thinking to myself that someday when I get older and wiser, I might write a book that could show younger people what actually happens after they sell their used textbooks back to the college book store (I don't even know if this is done anymore). Well, folks, someday is here, and if you deem this book to be half as enlightening as I did Mr. McCormack's book, I will then, and only then, think of myself as a writer and consider this effort worthwhile. The original working title for this book was The Accidental Combover because, like most people in the property management industry, I didn't tell my high school guidance counselor that I wanted to be a commercial property manager when I graduated from college. Rather, I fell into this industry quite accidentally. The combover part came from the fact that I realized I had a bald spot on the top of my head, and the way I have been parting my hair for years was covering it without my knowledge until recently!

I started a moving and storage business called Brewer & Son while still in college at the New York Institute of Technology on Long Island and enjoyed a small degree of success with it for about twelve years. In 1992, I sold the business and moved to the Tampa area with my wife and two young sons. I put a down payment on a to-be-constructed house and was so naïve that I didn't realize that one needs a job to show income in order to qualify for a mortgage. Out of necessity, I got a job with the local North American Van Lines agency as a sales manager, that I talk about in Chapter 1. I knew I didn't want to go back into the moving business, but it was the only occupation I was qualified for that would pay enough for me to qualify for the mortgage I needed.

Immediately after college and while I was still starting up the moving business, but before I was convinced that I could actually make a living from it, I worked as an assistant manager at a rollerskating rink in Massapequa, NY, called United Skates of America. I lasted all of five weeks, mostly because, well, I was an assistant manager of a rollerskating rink. I then was hired as an assistant manager at a W&J Sloane furniture store in Commack, NY. I lasted seven months there and was asked not to return because I gave a discount to an employee's mother, which I had seen the manager do without consequences, but apparently, this was not OK for me to do. I applied for unemployment and got it. I am still around, and W&J Sloane is not. I am not sure what that means, but it felt good writing it!

It was at this point that I decided to devote all of my efforts to Brewer & Son, as my track record outside of the moving business wasn't off to a great start, and I felt I the need to prove to my wife (we married three months after I graduated college) that I was actually capable of holding a job long term. The rest, as they say, is history.

Career Chronology and Markets Where I Had Asset Oversight; Designations and Awards

October 1982   Assistant Manager, United Skates of America Massapequa, NY

1983 - Assistant Store Manager, W&J Sloane Commack, NY

1980–1992 - Owner, Brewer & Son Moving and Storage Oceanside, NY

1992–1994 - Vice-President of Sales, North American Van Lines agency Tampa, FL

1995–1998 - Property Manager, The Wilson Company Tampa, FL Tampa, FL

1998 - Received RPA Designation from BOMA (Building Owners and Managers Association)

1998-2002 - Senior Property Manager, Florida Real Estate Advisors/Advantis Tampa, FL

2002-Received CPM Designation from IREM (Institute of Real Estate Management)

1995-2002 - Member BOMA Tampa

1997–2002 - BOMA Tampa Board of Directors

2000 - Property Manager of the Year, BOMA Tampa

2001 - Property Manager of the Year, BOMA Tampa

2002–2005 - Senior Asset Manager, Delma Properties St. Petersburg, FL

- St. Petersburg, FL
- Baltimore, MD
- Pembrooke Pines, FL
- Los Angeles, CA
- Boston, MA

2005–2008 - Regional Vice-President, IPC US REIT/Behringer Harvard St. Petersburg, FL

- St. Petersburg, FL
- Tampa, FL
- Weston, FL
- Wichita, KS
- Dallas, TX
- Houston, TX
- Baltimore, MD

2009–2011 - Vice-President of Operations, Colonial Properties Trust Lake Mary, FL

- Tampa, FL
- Lake Mary, FL
- Jacksonville, FL
- Heathrow, FL
- Clearwater, FL
- Orlando, FL
- Ft. Lauderdale, FL

2010 - Received CCIM Designation from the CCIM Institute (Certified Commercial Investment Member)

2011–2024 - Senior Managing Director, In-Rel Properties/Morning Calm Management LLC Boca Raton, FL

- Tampa, FL
- Jacksonville, FL
- Port Charlotte, FL
- West Palm Beach, FL
- South FL (assets in multiple markets)
- Birmingham, AL
- Oklahoma City, OK
- Memphis, TN
- Nashville, TN
- Lexington, KY

- Columbia, SC
- DMV (District of Columbia/Maryland/N. Virginia) – (assets in multiple markets)
- Philadelphia, PA
- Dallas, TX
- Detroit, MI
- Cleveland, Ohio
- Minneapolis, Minn.

Note: Job titles reflect the title I had when I left that particular company.

Since I started traveling in 2002, I have accumulated over 1500 nights with the Marriott Hotel chain, along with millions of Marriott points. This may sound cool and exciting, but anyone who has traveled for business for over 20 years will tell you it is nothing to brag about. I retired March 8, 2024, and the last five years (at least) of travel have been an absolute grind. Many times, I have got to my hotel room after work, called my wife, returned emails and crashed before 8 PM. I would wake up before midnight, look at my cell phone and think, "Oh crap. It is still Tuesday!" I do not miss traveling one bit.

Chapter 1
"I Don't Know the Difference Between a Chiller and a Volkswagen Bus"

That is what I told Gary Welch with The Wilson Company during an informational interview he granted me in early 1995, and I immediately regretted saying it. I was working for a North American Van Lines agency in Tampa as Vice-President of Sales, and I hated it. A good friend of mine named Hilary Becker, a successful real estate professional in his own right on Long Island, suggested I try and break into the commercial real estate business as I was already in BOMA (Building Owners and Managers Association) as a vendor and since I had already met a bunch of local commercial property managers at the monthly lunch meetings, my network was in place. Nina Gang, the executive director of BOMA Tampa at the time, set up the meeting with Gary with the purpose of simply being able to see if my skillset could transfer from the moving and storage industry to the commercial property management business.

The meeting was supposed to last 15 minutes, and after 45 minutes, I asked Gary if he was thinking of hiring me. He said he was, and that is when I confidently told him that I didn't know the difference between a chiller and a Volkswagen bus. He just stared at me for what seemed like two minutes but was probably more like two seconds and finally said, "I can teach you that, but I can't teach you motivation, desire, attitude, personality, common sense and determination, and you seem to have all of these attributes."

I worked at The Wilson Company with Gary for three years and he, along with Larry Finch, taught me the fundamentals of commercial real estate management that are embedded in my DNA to this day. Some of these pearls include:

- You get what you inspect, not what you expect.
- Every day is lease renewal day.
- The property manager is the mayor of his/her building. He/she needs to walk the building and, shake hands and kiss babies.
- The tenants are our most prized possessions. They pay our salaries.

I created a PowerPoint presentation on tenant relations based on these core values and others I picked up along the way, and it is discussed in some detail in Chapter 12.

Chapter 2
"The Building Doesn't Have Enough Plumbing for Medical Use"

From 2002 through about 2005, I had a portfolio of office buildings in the San Fernando Valley area of Los Angeles. One of the buildings on Ventura Blvd had an outbuilding consisting of approximately 8,000 square feet. I was the asset manager for Delma Properties at the time, and property management, leasing and construction all reported to me. Sometime in probably 2004, we had this 8,000 square foot space just about leased to ReMax Real Estate. Most terms were agreed upon but the lease was not signed yet. I was sitting in my office in St. Petersburg, FL, one day, and I get a phone call that goes something like this.

Ring

Me: "Doug Brewer speaking."

Charles: "Hi. My name is Charles White, and I am the business manager for Dr. Dre. We love the location of the building you have for lease on Ventura Blvd. in Woodland Hills, and we want to lease it from you".

It is at this point that I must caution you to swallow any food or drink that may be in your mouth.

Me: "That building doesn't have enough plumbing for medical use"

Charles: (After a long pause) "Dr. Dre is a Hip Hop artist, not an actual doctor."

Me: "Oh….(there was a long pause on my part because I didn't know what to say) ….We almost have the space leased to another company".

Charles: "We will pay you double the rent the other group was going to pay you, and we will do our own buildout without expecting you to contribute."

Me: (Somewhat sarcastically and with a large amount of skepticism) "I will need a ten-year term and will need Mr. Dre to sign for the lease personally and will need personal financials as well as company financials. I assume this will be a recording studio?"

Charles: "We agree to all of your terms, and we will be using the building as a private health club to get actors and actresses in shape for their upcoming roles in films. Our clients include Brittany Spears, Sylvester Stallone and Halle Berry." These three people I HAD heard of.

About a week later, I flew to L.A., lease in hand, and go to the address Charles gave me. It was in a nondescript shopping center about a block away from our building. It wasn't impressive from the front, but when I went around back as instructed, I saw a parking lot filled with high-end cars. I walked into an upscale gym, and Dr. Dre was sitting on the bench by the door with an extremely attractive woman. The only other celebrities I had seen by chance up to that point were Soupy Sales and the guy who always played Woody Allen's best friend in many of his movies, so I was a little star-struck and apparently stared at the couple a little too long as Charles quickly appeared to usher me away to an office. We ironed out some remaining minor business points and Charles assured me that Dr. Dre would sign the lease and he/Charles would return it to me along with Dr. Dre's personal financial statement.

A week went by, and I still hadn't received anything, so I called Charles, who told me that Dr. Dre was in the middle of recording an album with Fiddy Cent and he works from approximately 6:00 PM through 6:00 AM and had given orders not to be disturbed while he was sleeping during the day unless the house was on fire. I never knew Charles to stutter, so I asked him if 50 Cents was a person. After Charles explained to me that Fiddy Cent was also a rap artist, it sounded reasonable, and in another week, the signed lease and personal income statement came in the mail (this was 2004, don't forget). We countersigned, and the deal was done. I know the work started on the space, but I left Delma Properties before it was completed. Unfortunately, I had no further communication with Charles or Dr. Dre, as I am sure I could have learned a lot as both proved to have a high business acumen.

Chapter 3
"Do What You Say You are Going to Do"

From about 2004 through 2007, I had a portfolio of multi-tenant office and retail buildings in Wichita, Kansas, when I worked for IPC US REIT. They were a publicly traded company on the Canadian stock exchange with corporate headquarters in Toronto and US headquarters in Louisville, KY. One of the buildings in Wichita was in the Central Business District, and it was the tallest building in the downtown – 23 stories, I believe. The name of the building was Epic Center. As with Delma Properties, I had property management, leasing and construction management reporting to me for my portion of the total portfolio.

There was a one or two-floor (I can't remember the exact size of the prospect, but it was big for Wichita) law firm that was in the market to potentially move out of the second tallest building in downtown Wichita, and they had narrowed down their choices to Epic Center and the building they were currently in. The incumbent building, by the way, was owned by a gentleman who also owned a casino resort hotel in Vegas, although I forget the guy's name and the name of the casino. This fact has nothing to do with the point of this story but is just an interesting aside.

Both our third-party broker, our paralegal in Louisville and I spent a great deal of time reviewing proposals and drafting counter-proposals, as well as meeting with the managing partner of the law firm and the other decision-makers. Everyone we met at the firm seemed to be a sincere and honorable person with a good deal of both common and business sense. I remember always looking forward to our interactions – electronically, by phone and in-person.

They made the decision to remain where they were, and the managing partner assured me that it was a tough decision made tougher by the professional way both my third-party broker and I conducted ourselves. I thanked him for the kind words, and while disappointed that we didn't get the deal, I was satisfied that we did everything we could have done without any regrets.

A few days later, I was in my office in St. Petersburg, FL (yes, same building; IPC had purchased the asset from Delma, and after a few months, I accepted an offer to join IPC. The running joke was that I was like the office furniture – I was included in the deal!) when I received a phone call from the managing partner of the law firm, he asked me if our latest offer was still on the table, and I told him it was. He asked me to send him the lease, and he would sign it and return it to me. After I thanked him and made some small talk, I asked him if he would mind telling me what changed his mind. He said that when he received the final version of the renewal document from his current landlord, the starting rent was increased by $.25 per square foot from the agreed-upon final Letter of Intent. He said that in the Midwest, a man is only as good as his word, and a handshake is his bond. He signed the lease and moved into Epic Center.

Obviously, I never forgot that encounter, and if I commit to do something, you can rest assured that I will do it.

Chapter 4
The Definition of Management

When I graduated college in June 1982, the country was in the midst of a recession, I was told. I still wasn't convinced that I could make a living with my part-time moving business or if I even wanted to, so I was scouring the help-wanted ads in Newsday and the NY Times each Sunday looking for that perfect job. For you Gen X'ers and Millennials reading this, there were no home computers yet, so we had to use newspapers to get information. After my five-week stint as king of the rollerskating rink, I got an interview to manage the afore mentioned W&J Sloane store. At the time, W&J Sloane was one of the most prestigious and recognized furniture stores in NY. I found out that, due to the recession, there were over 100 applicants for this position. Somehow, I was granted an interview, and I found myself sitting across the desk of a Mr. Firestone, one of the company's vice-presidents. He was probably in his 60s, and I was all of 22 years old so we naturally had a lot in common.

At some point, he asked me for my definition of management, and my confidence and bravado level soared. Afterall, I had just graduated from the prestigious NY Institute of Technology with a BS in Business Management and could wax poetic on all things personnel management theory related. I started reciting excerpts from my textbooks by BF Skinner, Peter Drucker and Frederick Winslow Taylor when he put his hand up to stop me. He said, "Kid, the definition of management is getting work done through other people." It felt like a baseball bat to the kneecaps; it was so humbling. It was also so 1960's and 1970's management. Obviously, there is a lot more to management than this, but an element of his simple definition still rings true some 42 years later. Also, he hired me, so he must have been quite wise.

At its core, management is quite simple…until it has to be put into practice.

Chapter 5
"After 10 Years, She's a F**king Florist!"

I had an approximately 200,000 square-foot multi-tenant office building in downtown Columbia, South Carolina, on Gervais St from about 2012–2014, where we engaged the local Colliers agency to manage and lease it for us. We started out with a terrific leasing broker and property manager, and I would visit the asset quarterly from my office in Tampa when I worked at In-Rel Properties. At these quarterly visits, I would first meet with the team in the conference room, and we would start out by discussing all relevant matters related to property management, leasing and construction before we would tour the building and possibly tour the market as well.

At one meeting, in probably late 2013, we all sat down in the conference room as usual, but this time, I noticed that our leasing broker looked nervous. The vice-president of the Colliers agency joined us for this meeting and, after some pleasantries, informed me of what she termed "exciting news." The property manager was being promoted to something like assistant vice-president and a new property manager would be starting in about two weeks who actually had worked for this Colliers agency before. I congratulated the property manager, who I was legitimately happy for as she was doing a great job at my building, and I thought the promotion was well-deserved. I asked to see the resume of the new property manager and said that I would like to meet her or him before I gave my blessing, but since they already knew this person and recommended her, my approval was likely just a formality. Or so I thought.

It was at this time that I looked over at the broker and again noticed that he looked even more nervous than when we originally sat down. The vice-president slid the resume of the incoming property manager across the table to me, and the broker began shuffling his leasing update sheets rather loudly. The most recent job on this lady's resume indicated that she worked as a florist for the last ten years! I thought about what to say next without sounding like a jerk, but I was incapable of doing so. "Let me get this straight. You are recommending to me that a florist manage my $30 million dollar office building?" This struck me as so preposterous that it was almost funny if it wasn't so outlandish and an insult to my intelligence. Visions of this being part of a Monty Python or Seinfeld episode flashed through my mind.

The vice-president started to tell me that this person was an excellent property manager and had to use the latest version of Excel in her current job as a florist when I cut her off by saying something like, "Not happening, and please stop talking." I explained to her that ten years, a decade for pete's sake, was a long time and technology changes drastically in 3 years, much less ten. When the vice-president attempted to rebut my rationale, I stood up and said in an elevated tone, "After ten years, she is a F**king florist." They kept the incumbent property manager for another six months or so and replaced her with someone who was actually working in property management.

I rarely drop the F-bomb, but I am only human. The lesson here is, when the time comes to drop the hammer, do it. Don't wait or you will appear weak or will appear to have less conviction than what you actually have.

Chapter 6
"That's One Way to Solve a Problem"

My first property management assignment was managing Bayport Plaza by Tampa International Airport. Bayport Plaza is a class A twelve-story 263,000 square foot multi-tenant office building with many Fortune 500 tenants and shares a peninsula that juts out into Tampa Bay with the Hyatt Hotel. The Wilson Company's corporate office was there, and I received all the support I needed from a bunch of truly wonderful people. Again, thank you, Gary, Larry and Barry (Hanerfeld).

There was a balcony on the fourth floor off the Dun & Bradstreet space that was lined with planters and had some outdoor furniture. It overlooked the plaza area and was essentially over front doors to the office building and hotel with cars having to access this area to enter the parking garage. The problem with the balcony was it was inundated with pigeons, dozens of them. The Wilson Company had tried for years to rid the balcony of pigeons to no avail. They tried installing razor wire on the ledge of the planters, sprinkling a product I think was called Hot Feet on the paver floor and installing a plastic crow in hopes of scaring away these rats with wings. Apparently, pigeons are smarter than we give them credit for, as well as somewhat vindictive as they pooped all over the plastic crow as well as everywhere else on the balcony.

I was discussing this issue with our pest control vendor and he suggested poison corn. I don't believe this is legal today in Florida, but in 1996, I was told it was. His plan was to sprinkle untainted corn on the balcony for three Saturdays in a row and then, on the fourth Saturday, sprinkle the poison corn. He said it was a humane way to kill the birds. He was mistaken. I want to make it clear that I deeply regret this decision and wished it never happened. If I had it to do over, I would have just let the birds remain and simply pressure-washed the balcony regularly, even though this was only marginally effective.

After the first week of sprinkling the regular corn, it appeared the varmints were calling their cousins in Sarasota to come and enjoy the feast. By the third installment of free food, you would have thought a Golden Corral for pigeons had opened on the balcony, as the pigeon population in the immediate area seemed to have increased tenfold.

On the fourth Saturday, my work cell phone rang at about 10:00 in the morning, and I was greeted by a very angry and flustered Hyatt general manager. All I could make out from his initial pass at conversation after he started by saying, "What the hell did you do?" were phrases like, "dive-bombing into the pool" and "guests demanding their money back." I assured him I didn't know what he was referring to when he let go a string of profanities that would make a sailor blush. He told me that his maintenance staff had already bagged over 20 dead pigeons, and they were falling from the sky. I thanked him for letting me know and reminded him that we needed to continue to work together and that I would look into the matter on Monday.

On Monday morning, as I was riding the elevator to our office, our director of accounting was riding with me and looked quite pale, almost ashen. I asked her if she was OK and she said there were three dead pigeons in her parking space. A few moments later, I sheepishly went into my boss's office to let him know what transpired over the weekend and before I could say anything, he said to me without looking up from his desk, "That's one way to solve a problem".

Sometimes, you have to just take your shot by thinking outside the box, however, do your homework first. In retrospect, I should have asked more questions of my pest control guy before I agreed to the treatment.

Chapter 7
Mentorship

The word 'Mentor' is thrown around too frequently, in my opinion, these days. The three people I mentioned at the beginning of this book were mentors of mine and I would never be so presumptuous to include myself in the same breath as them as it relates to success and intelligence. However, there were times in my career that I may have had a positive impact on the career of people who reported to me.

I am including three emails I received from three younger individuals I worked with for different periods of time. These emails hang on the wall in my home office and are a constant reminder that helping the people who report to you to achieve their goals and unashamedly pushing them to make them into the best professional version of themselves is truly the way to approach each work day. I didn't realize this until much later in my career, but understanding this later in one's career is better than never understanding it at all. Receiving these letters truly is among the highlights of my life.

I know they thank me in their emails, but I should be the one thanking each of them for making it easy to look forward to coming to work each day. I know there were others who might use the M-word when talking about me, but these three people put their thoughts in writing and I thought I would share them with you. Yes, it is personal, and yes, I may be patting myself on the back a little, but if this inspires even one reader to go to work each day with the main goal of helping the people he or she works with to become a better real estate professional, I will gladly accept the raised eyebrows.

Nothing has given me more satisfaction in my property management career than seeing young people who have worked for me advance and achieve things they previously didn't think possible and knowing that I may have had even a small part in their success.

Hi Doug,

I was thinking of you today and wanted to give you an update on where I'm at in life. Not because I am looking for a response or praise, but because I wanted to express my gratitude to you.

Today I put in my two weeks-notice at my current job. After a year of working with a "chair manager" I realized that you, and managers of your caliber, are few and far between. I want you to know that you are an excellent manager of people. You are honest, approachable and greatly motivated me when I was at MCM to reach my full potential. You always offered to help, no matter the issue, and you always answered my calls- or called me back even if it was a few hours later. You worked harder than any of your property managers/staff and I respected you greatly for it. I know you care, and it shows. There's not many like you out there, and I hope you know you have raised the bar for me. My expectations of leaders and mentors are forever changed.

Anyways I hope you are having a wonderful summer and are out at concerts with your family and getting some much needed rest and relaxation.

Thank you again for everything.

Hi Doug,

I hope this email finds you well. I wanted to write to say, Thank You. I appreciate the time and effort you put aside to help my development. Leadership is not about titles. It is about one life influencing another. It is an action not a position. I have grown so much these past 9 months both personally and professionally because of your leadership. You have been a tremendous help, a great mentor and motivator for me. You inspired me with your strength and resilience. I am forever grateful to have met you and worked alongside you.

I know I will take the lessons you have taught with me wherever I go. (and there were many lessons) I don't think I can truly put on paper the impact you've had on my life. I know my leaving was abrupt but I believe everything happens for a reason. Everything in its time and its season. There are no mistakes.

I wish you all the best. I hope you get some rest and take a proper vacation with no phones ☺

Again, thank you for everything!

Hi Doug,

Thank you so much for this thoughtful email. I want to express my heartfelt gratitude for your continuous support and words of encouragement. Your guidance and mentorship have been invaluable to me throughout the years, especially considering my limited knowledge of property management when I first started. You have always been an exceptional boss, consistently believing in me and offering unwavering support in every situation.

I am immensely grateful for always having my back, regardless of the challenges I faced. The lessons learned have and continue to be instrumental in shaping my professional journey. Just like you, during your early days in property management, I am certain that the lessons you imparted will remain ingrained in my memory. I am committed to sharing those valuable lessons with others, as you have done with me.

Lately, I have found myself experiencing heightened emotions as I approach this transition. I have genuinely cherished my role in property management, making it difficult to let go of the responsibilities I have held. Parting ways with my team is particularly difficult as they have become an integral part of my daily life. Nevertheless, I am determined to bring the knowledge and expertise I have acquired as a property manager to my new position. My aspiration is to fill the void that exists in the construction sector of South Florida and make a positive impact.

Once again, I want to extend my deepest appreciation for everything you have done for me over the years. Your belief in my abilities has played a significant role in my professional development. I am truly grateful for the opportunities you have provided and the trust you have placed in me.

With sincere appreciation,

Chapter 8
"Because You Get S**t Done"

The first stop in my real estate career was with the Wilson Company in Tampa and it lasted three years before the building was sold and Wilson lost the management assignment. I made the tough but correct decision to stay at the building with the new management company even though I was offered a different position with Wilson. At one point, I thought my property management career might have been over after only a short time.

I had been with Wilson about six months, and I thought I was doing well, but I was starting from the bottom – literally with no knowledge of commercial property management (remember, chiller…VW bus!) whatsoever. My business card said I was the property manager, but my direct boss, Larry Finch, and awesome administrative assistant, Sandra McBride, were really the people running building operations. One morning, I came to find out that we lost the management assignment for one of the larger buildings in the portfolio and this building was managed by a seasoned and knowledgeable property manager. It was at this point when I reasoned that the prudent business decision to make was to let me go and put this experienced manager in charge of Bayport Plaza. This made so much sense to me, and likely to just about everyone else, that I remember telling my wife that I may be out of work soon but was hopeful to find another position in the property management industry, even though I had only minimal experience.

I also remember toying with the idea of just flat out asking the guy who hired me – senior vice-president Gary Welch – if, or when, he was going to replace me with this seasoned professional who, all of a sudden, had no building to manage. I resisted the urge to do so and actually tried to stay away from Gary and my direct boss, reasoning that if they couldn't find me, they couldn't let me go.

A few days later, I saw this seasoned professional cleaning out her desk, and I asked her what was going on. She told me that she was told that Wilson didn't have an opening for her, so they were letting her go. I mustered the self-control not to give myself a high five in front of her, instead saying how much help she had been to me (which was a lie) and that I was sure, with her credentials, she would find another job very shortly.

I was walking by Gary's office a day or two later when I saw him at his desk with the door open. I knocked and asked if he had a few minutes to chat. Curiosity had gotten the better of me, and I asked him why he kept me instead of the seasoned pro. His answer was, "Because you get S**t done."

From that moment on, getting stuff done TIMELY has always been worn on my sleeve. If you need to stay at work 30 minutes or an hour more than you usually do or need to stay longer than planned to finish a project or a report without leaving it for the next day, do it. You won't be sorry. My favorite word in the English language became "now." Mook Cho (CEO of Morning Calm Management) actually coined this phrase, and I am only borrowing it.

Always try to do more work today, as it will lessen the workload for tomorrow.

Chapter 9

"You Are Already Wet"

When I was the property manager at Bayport Plaza in Tampa, one of the lawyers in the building was also the mayor of a smaller city outside of Tampa. He was a true gentleman and was very well-respected in the community. One sunny afternoon after lunch, he was walking across the plaza from the parking garage to the building, and he chose the path that was adjacent to a large fountain comprised of several features, including a "pool" that was about six feet square and four feet deep. Around the perimeter of the pool was a polished granite surface that was known to be slippery, especially when wet. I think you see where I am going here.

Mr. Mayor slipped on the wet surface and fell into the pool. He was dressed in a suit and tie and was completely submerged. I came across the scene as he was climbing out of the pool, and I hurried towards him to offer assistance. Although embarrassed due to the many witnesses and rubbernecking (think car accident), he was laughing about it and pointed to his eyeglasses that remained under four feet of water. I had my maintenance engineer run next door to the Hyatt Hotel and get their pool skimmer which I used to try and retrieve the glasses. After a few attempts, I realized that there was a good chance that I would break the glasses as I had to pin them against the wall of the pool for leverage.

After about 30 seconds, the tenant/mayor and I looked at each other, and we both knew we were thinking the same thing. I told him with a shrug, "You are already wet" and he proceeded to ease himself back into the pool and completely submerge once again and pick up his glasses.

It was at this moment that the president of my management company happened to be walking by and asked me what our tenant was doing in the fountain. When I told him that he was retrieving his glasses, the president of my company simply looked at me with a 'I wish I never saw this' look and said, "OK," and kept walking. We got a bunch of towels from the Hyatt so the mayor could dry himself off, and all was good. The mayor had the need to call me a few years later and started the conversation by saying, "Hello, Doug. This is the guy who fell in the fountain!".

As stated earlier in the book, managing Bayport Plaza was my first job in commercial real estate management. I knew nothing about real estate when I started, but I knew a lot about customer relations from my moving business days. My first two to three weeks were spent visiting with each tenant (about 40 tenants total), passing out my business cards and getting the business cards of each person I met with so I could send them a 'thank you for meeting with me' email. I especially made it a point to meet with the receptionist, my tenant contact and the senior person in the office.

Because of the good working relationship I had developed with this tenant/mayor, the fountain incident was nothing more than an unfortunate and somewhat comical event that was soon forgotten. We did profile the slippery granite perimeter of the fountain shortly thereafter and I made sure to tell the tenant/mayor that we did this.

Building a strong professional relationship with your tenants can turn large issues into small ones and turn small issues into non-issues. The best commercial property management work is done in the field and not in the office.

Chapter 10
Bet on Yourself

When I first started with In-Rel Properties in 2011, I was told they were the second largest owner of office space in Memphis, behind Highwoods Properties, and I am not disputing this. We owned six multi-tenant office properties totaling about 1.5 million square feet, including Clark Tower, the largest building in Memphis. I spent my first two days with In-Rel in their Lake Worth, FL corporate office, meeting the staff and generally getting caught up on our properties around the country. The CEO, Mook Cho, had told me at one of our meetings before I accepted the position of senior vice-president of property management and construction that the Memphis office had a few issues and needed some leadership, and he reiterated that before I left for Memphis from our Lake Worth office on my third day with the company. It turned out that was like saying Jessie James may have robbed a few banks!

The week before I got to Memphis, the director of property management for the entire portfolio and the property manager for the Memphis portfolio were let go. I was told the former property manager committed to sleeping in the office, if he had to, during his interview….we just weren't aware he was referring to doing it during business hours! When I arrived in Memphis, the property management staff included two young and inexperienced tenant coordinators and an administrative assistant. That's it…for a 1.5 million square foot portfolio and over 200 tenants! Oh yeah, and the property manager for our Nashville portfolio had offered to start spending about half his time in Memphis to "help out."

The company's Memphis office in Clark Tower was essentially a long hallway with offices on either side, maybe 3,000 square feet total. At one end of the hallway was the leasing department, which consisted of a large office with a private restroom and 2-3 smaller offices. My leasing counterpart sat there. The other end of the hallway was for property management and laid out in a similar fashion, minus the private restroom.

I arrived at the Memphis office mid-morning on day three of my In-Rel adventure and started at the leasing end of the hallway, introducing myself as I went. I met the admin and the two tenant coordinators and all seemed like nice people just chomping at the bit for some real leadership and instruction in commercial property management. When I got to the large office at the end of the property management end of the hallway, the Nashville property manager was at the desk and had set up camp in this large office and appeared quite comfortable. After introducing ourselves and exchanging pleasantries, I asked him if he knew I was arriving today and he said quite confidently that he did know this as a fact. I then asked him what office he envisioned me having as the only vacant desk was an open space next to the front door with a desk that was nothing more than a small conference table with a few chairs.

He looked like I had asked him to explain Einstein's Theory of Relativity as he just stared blankly at me for a few seconds before muttering something akin to, "I don't know," and started to move his stuff to the open space by the front door. A few weeks later, I thanked him for his thoughtfulness in offering to assist at the Memphis office but told him to stay in Nashville and make sure he was doing the best job he possibly could, and I would be there at some point to assist and evaluate.

I met with the staff, including the chief engineer and his engineering staff, and told them a little bit about myself, what my expectations were and what I wanted to accomplish when the chief informed me that he and his engineers were not part of the property management team and reported to the director of construction now. More on this unusual response in the next chapter.

I then met with the two tenant coordinators, we identified the 10-12 largest tenants in the portfolio, and I asked them to schedule meetings with their tenant contacts and the highest-ranking person in that office over the next two weeks. It was apparent very quickly that I would be spending the majority of my time in Memphis over the next three to six months.

One of the other assets we owned in Memphis was called Lynfield, very likely because it was on, well, Lynfield St. It consisted of three two-story 75,000-square-foot office buildings. The Bank of Tennessee occupied two of the buildings, so that bank was definitely on my list of larger Memphis tenants. The two tenant coordinators essentially split the portfolio and the Lynfield tenant coordinator had made an appointment for us to meet with the office manager and the bank vice-president one morning the following week.

For the next six months, I would fly to Memphis from my home in the Tampa area on Monday morning and fly back to Tampa on Friday afternoon. This occurred just about every week while I neglected our properties in Tampa, South Florida, Oklahoma City,

Nashville, Columbia and Birmingham. Every Saturday, I would work out of our Tampa office to catch up on issues at these other properties from my previous week in Memphis.

The Lynfield tenant coordinator and I arrived at the bank's offices 15 minutes early (a good habit to get into) for our meeting, and we were brought into a nicely decorated conference room. After a few minutes, the office manager and bank vice president arrived with what appeared to be forced smiles on their faces. After introductions, the office manager started to say that she never once met the former property manager or the tenant coordinator who was sitting in front of her when the bank vice-president cut her off with a wave of his hand. I am paraphrasing because it occurred almost 13 years ago, but his message was essentially this.

"You calling yourselves a property management company is a joke. Your company couldn't manage their way out of a paper bag. Our phone calls don't get returned. You are nice enough to answer most of our emails, albeit days later, but no actions are ever taken regarding our requests. Communication is virtually non-existent, and work orders never get completed on time, if they get completed at all. The janitorial staff has no direction, there are bugs and mice in our space, the landscaping looks like hell, although I will give you credit for the grass being cut timely, and salt is never applied to our parking lot and front steps when there is an ice storm. Every time I see your property management fee included in my CAM statements, I feel like I am being robbed at gunpoint. I want a lease amendment that removes our requirement to pay your property management fee, and we will manage the buildings ourselves".

I was quiet for a moment before I spoke. I told him that this was my second week, and I agreed our report card was a capital F. I told him that he would see improvement starting that evening and that we would be improving each week and, if by the end of the year, four short months away, he didn't give us an A grade, I would have a lease amendment drafted removing the bank's requirement to pay a management fee and allow them to manage the building themselves. Mind you, I did a quick calculation in my head of what the property management fee might be, and I was betting $90,000 annually on myself. 150,000 square feet x $20 per square foot x 3% management fee = $90K.

I remember getting on a virtual meeting with the CEO and one of the other two owners of In-Rel that afternoon and relaying the highlights of my meeting that morning with the bank. When I got to the part about my promise to forgo the management fee if the bank didn't feel we were an A rated property management firm in four months, they just looked at me without saying anything for what seemed like an eternity. At some point, I simply moved on to the next topic and the meeting ended without comment from either of them on my commitment.

This is the action plan I put in place in an attempt to get that A rating and likely save my job.

1. That same day, the tenant coordinator and I met with the owner of the janitorial company and had a come-to-Jesus meeting. The outcome of this meeting had the janitorial foreman meeting with the tenant coordinator each afternoon to review any complaints or special cleaning that was needed. I considered strongly changing janitorial companies just to

show the bank that there was a new sheriff in town, but that first inspection revealed that they were actually keeping the building clean with no direction from us.
2. Every morning for two weeks, the tenant coordinator, the janitorial supervisor, the maintenance engineer for that building and I would walk the space from top to bottom, flush every toilet, inspect every utility room and check in with the office manager.
3. The tenant coordinator would check in with the office manager every morning for the next four months, whether there was anything to discuss or not. I just wanted the bank to know we were there and cared.
4. The tenant coordinator and I would review the list of work orders weekly to make sure all were closed out and do pop-in follow-ups to make sure the work orders were actually completed.
5. When we got to the roof on the first full building inspection, we saw that the trees around the buildings were so overgrown that the tips of the branches were just about touching the roof. This was a ready-made rodent and pest entre to the building. I had the landscapers out that week to trim back all the trees and install new plants and flowers at the front entrance for an immediate first impression upgrade.
6. I noticed several pest control entries per week for $99 each for the last year or so on the general ledger, amounting to almost $1,000 monthly. When I asked to see the pest control contract, the tenant coordinator informed me there wasn't one, which was the reason for all the charges. This was a pretty sweet set up for the pest control company, kind of like an annuity or the gift that keeps on giving. The management company allows

the trees to grow onto the roof, creating a never-ending rodent and bug problem, necessitating a need for the pest control company to continuously be called out. With no contract in place, the pest control company is able to charge for each visit. I felt like I was back in New York with my moving business, continually having to tip the elevator operator of the office building to take us up to the floor!

7. I met with the pest control company and asked them how much the kickback was they were giving to the former property manager and they got offended. I asked why there was no contract in place, and their answer was essentially, "If the management company is so dumb as to allow us to charge for multiple visits per week over an extended period of time, we will gladly continue to do so and bill." I thanked them for their honesty and never called them again. I believe the appropriate term here is, 'They are dead to me.' I brought in a new pest control company that week, and after charging me something like $1,000 for an initial treatment, their monthly charge was $99 per month for unlimited visits (within reason)!

I was spending so much time in Memphis that I was on a first-name basis with the lady who ran the takeout window at the Olive Garden next to Clark Tower, and the front desk people at the local Marriott Courtyard would smile and say, "See you Monday, have a nice weekend," as I dropped off my room access card each Friday morning.

As the calendar drew closer to December, my angst increased. My Memphis staff was clicking on all cylinders, and our vendors were doing what we contracted them to do, with the threat of me invoking the 30-day termination clause in their contracts fresh in their minds. I knew we were putting forth an A rated effort, but it didn't matter what I thought; the litmus test was the bank's perception. When December arrived, I was hesitant to approach the office manager and vice president, so I never did. I simply continued to make sure my people were doing what they were supposed to do, and I never heard another word from the bank.

Putting $100 on black at a casino in Vegas is gambling. Betting on yourself within reason is as close to a sure thing as you can get.

Chapter 11
The Single Worst Decision Witnessed in My Property Management Career

Thankfully, this decision wasn't made by me. In the last chapter, I mentioned that the chief engineer in Memphis informed me that he and his maintenance engineers no longer were part of the property management department and now reported to the director of construction. When I asked the chief if this made sense to him, he got an uncomfortable look on his face and he said it did not and it was never this way at other companies he had worked for. I thanked him for his honesty and asked who made this decision. I like asking questions when I already know the answer, and this was one of those questions. His answer was that it was the director of construction. I reminded him that the director of construction reported to me and that I would be getting back to him on this matter shortly.

The director of construction officed out of our Birmingham office and drove to Memphis that first week to meet with me. He was a younger guy who was an Army Ranger in Afghanistan and Iraq. I thanked him for his service and immediately dove into his rationale for staging what amounted to a partial coup d'etat. He started waxing poetic on how this was the best move for the company, and it will take some of the burden off me, and that is when I couldn't take his bullshit anymore and asked him to stop talking. I said it seemed to me that he did this because he could. The former director of property management was scared to make a mistake and was making decisions out of fear. He saw an opportunity to stroke his own ego by seizing more power, and he took it. I asked him if my hypothesis was close and he glared at me for a few minutes and then, to his credit, admitted that I had hit the bullseye. He also admitted that he really didn't even know what property managers actually did.

I told him that this decision made absolutely no sense and was possibly the single worst decision I had ever encountered in my 16 years in the commercial property management business up to that point. I told him that the goal of the construction department is to build out spaces on time and on budget, while the goal of the engineering team is to ensure that the building systems are operating correctly and the tenants have a safe and comfortable environment in which to work in. I told him that these are also some of the goals of the property manager and that the engineering team is logically an extension of property management.

Sometimes, it is necessary to cut someone who reports to you off at the kneecaps like this, but it is also critical to understand that if you want to retain that person, you need to build them up again, which is what I tried to do over the next couple of years that we worked together. It turned out that working with this guy was a struggle for me almost every day and he eventually left to take a job in, believe it or not, property management! I do want to say that he is a good guy and that I wish him nothing but happiness and success.

Chapter 12

Core Beliefs of Highly Successful Property Management Teams

I have attended over one hundred BOMA and IREM lunches and property management seminars in my career, but I don't recall a single one being on the subject of tenant relations. I never understood that, as tenants pay our salaries or at least assist in funding them. That is why I decided to create a presentation on tenant relations. From 2009-2011, I worked for a REIT with corporate headquarters in Birmingham called Colonial Properties Trust. Colonial was a larger multi-family REIT that also happened to own about 13 million square feet of office and retail product, mostly in the southeast part of the United States. Shortly before I got there, Colonial sold an 85% share of its commercial properties to a group out of New York called DRA. My responsibility was the oversight of property management for the six million square feet of office and retail product owned by this joint venture in Florida.

My tenure at Colonial was during the Great Recession so the focus on retaining existing tenants, as well as watching every dollar we spent, was our top priority. This mindset triggered my motivation to create a PowerPoint presentation I called Core Beliefs of Highly Effective Property Management Teams. A special thanks here to my assistant and office manager with Colonial, Colleen Maguire, who put the presentation together for me. By the way, I brought Colleen with me to In-Rel Properties/Morning Calm Management, and she enjoyed a ten-year career there before relocating outside of Florida. She remains a close friend and confidant to this day.

I have presented this PowerPoint 15-20 times over the years, mostly to managers within the companies I was at, but would be happy to present to any group, anywhere, who feels they would benefit from a focused thought process on how the property management staff plays a critical role in retaining tenants and renewing leases.

These Core Beliefs are listed here, along with some bullet-pointed color on why I feel each one should be part of the successful commercial property manager's toolbelt. There are stories to go along with each bullet point but I will save those for future in-person or virtual presentations.

1. The Tenant is Our Most Prized Possession – They Pay Our Salaries

    - I could make the argument that keeping a tenant happy is the only goal of a property manager while everything else we do is simply a subset of this one goal.
    - Common sense – If someone gives me money, I tend to treat them pretty darn good.
    - Without tenants, property managers likely wouldn't have a job.

- A servant's heart

2. Property Management is a Service Business

    - We don't manufacture widgets or sell insurance; we sell our management services and ourselves every day.

3. Every day is Lease Renewal Day

    - The leasing team may wait to start the renewal process 6 months prior to lease expiration, but we, as property managers, need to start the renewal process on day one.

4. You Get What You Inspect, Not What You Expect

    - I expect the janitorial staff to empty the trash cans under each desk every night, but how do I know they are actually doing this unless and until I do a visual sampling of different tenants on different floors?
    - I expect each toilet to flush in my building, but how do I know until I actually push down the handle or depress the button?
    - I am an engineer who just responded to a hot call. I think I made the complaining tenant more comfortable, but how do I really know unless I go back to see him 20 minutes later and inquire? The follow-up may be the single most neglected part of a management team's job.

5. VPAC

    - Visitation – The property manager is the mayor of his or her building. He or she needs to shake hands and kiss babies.

    - Property Appearance – Dead landscaping and an overflowing trash can at the building's main entrance give guests and visitors a negative perception of the building and the management team.

    - Communication – Tenants can accept bad news and change if it is effectively communicated to them, much better than if it is rolled out with no advance notice.

6. Never Say No to a Tenant Unless You Have a Really Good Reason

    - If you have to deny a tenant request, make darn sure you can articulate that reason as clearly and as succinctly as possible.

    - Offer alternative solutions.

7. Outstanding Tenant Service is not a Big Thing; it is a Thousand Little Things.

    - Every commercial property management company does the big things right or they wouldn't be in business.

- They make sure the trash is removed each night, and they keep the building climate comfortable.

- It's doing the little things that show a tenant the management company cares and are memorable as the lease gets negotiated.

- Henry Kissinger said that leadership "…is the subtle accumulation of nuances, a hundred things done a little better."

8. The CEO, President and Vice-President are not the Most Important People in the Company.

    - Your building engineers are. They are the individuals who interact with our most prized possessions/tenants every day. Tenants can, and often do, form their opinion of the management company based on the engineers, as these are the people they see most often to correct operational issues.

    - Empower them to make on-the-spot monetary decisions up to a pre-determined threshold.

9. The Property Management Staff Should be Transparent and Blend into the Fabric of the Tenant Community

    - The goals of the property management staff should always be proactive. We should strive to identify issues and resolve them before the tenant even knows these issues exist.

- The goal should be no service calls

10. It's Not About the Buildings

    - This one strays from the tenant relations arena but is critical to property management teams nonetheless.

    - Your building is simply a conduit to you being a successful manager and leader – it doesn't define you.

    - Your work ethic, drive and integrity do.

11. Every Tenant Interaction Should be Viewed as an Interview and an Opportunity

    - Think back to the last time you interviewed for a job and how prepared you were in all phases – knowledge of the company, clothing, promptness, etc. A tenant meeting should be no different.

12. The Most Important Tenant in your Portfolio is the One You are Currently Speaking to or Emailing

    - I have done an entire seminar on how to write an email to a tenant – It is that important.

    - A tenant meeting is not a dress rehearsal (neither is life, for that matter); there are no second chances.

Chapter 13
Firing Someone

Over the course of my career, I have fired dozens of people. This is not something I am proud of, and it is not something I ever looked forward to, and am simply stating this as a fact. I have fired people for all sorts of reasons ranging from incompetence to stealing from the company to sexual harassment of tenants and fellow employees.

The sexual harassment cases are always interesting. I have had two, and both guys insisted on their innocence until the end, even when the evidence against them was overwhelming. One involved a body-building former marine who coincidentally scheduled his fountain cleaning with his short-sleeved uniform shirt sleeves rolled up to accentuate his biceps at 8:30 each morning when tenants were walking past the fountain to get from the parking garage to the office building. One CEO in the building told me that he had an affair with her (the CEO) receptionist, and he is not taking kindly to the receptionist's wish to end their relationship. He was also allegedly making advances towards the admin from a Fortune 500 company in the building, and they had their in-house investigator fly from their corporate office in Dallas to do some reconnaissance. The in-house investigator got the local police department involved, and when they approached me with their findings, I got my human resources department involved, and I terminated his employment. The last thing he said to me was, "What am I going to tell my wife?". I told him I was confident he would think of something.

When I was with IPC, the Canadian REIT, we acquired a class A hi-rise 300,000 square foot multi-tenant office building in downtown Baltimore where I needed to hire an entirely new staff as the seller had room for all their employees at other buildings they owned locally. One of the people I hired was an administrative assistant, who was a wonderful woman with little relevant experience who tried hard and proved to be a solid employee. Whenever I came to town, she would make me her "world famous" pineapple upside-down cake, which she proudly boasted contained three full bars of butter. It was delicious, although I thought I felt my arteries clogging after eating a piece at 9:30 in the morning, when I would typically arrive after taking the first flight out of Tampa.

In late 2007, I believe, IPC sold its assets to Behringer Harvard, a privately held REIT based in Dallas, and I was laid off toward the end of 2008, along with about 30 of my former IPC associates, due to the Great Recession. Fast forward about 10 years to 2017, and I am at Morning Calm Management, and we acquire the same Class A asset I had with IPC in downtown Baltimore. One of our acquisition philosophies at Morning Calm was that we need to operate the asset more efficiently than the seller or why acquire the asset at all? Some of the strategies we included were completing 'front of house' capital projects to enhance our new leasing and tenant retention efforts and reducing operating expenses by rebidding contracts, revisiting staffing size, doing a deep dive into the run times of major equipment, etc. After reviewing the staffing during due diligence, I made the decision that this truly wonderful woman, who was now an assistant property manager, was not essential to the operation of the property and that we would not be retaining her services once we closed on the asset. On one of my trips to Baltimore to tour the asset during due diligence, my intention was to make the staff offers to remain with the building and become employees of Morning Calm Management, except for this wonderful woman. Someone must have tipped her off that I was arriving that day because when I arrived, she had a pineapple upside-down cake waiting for me. How does one human being tell another human being that their services will no longer be needed when staring at a homemade pineapple upside-down cake made specifically for them? I am not ashamed to admit that I just couldn't do it.....that day. I extended my trip by a day and gave her the news the following day. She took it with her usual grace, and I truly hope she is doing well today.

Another time that proved to be even more awkward was when I fired an assistant property manager at around 4 PM due to incompetence. A few hours later, I was approaching a checkout line at a nearby Publix without paying much attention to the people around me when I saw that the person whose employment I had just terminated was doing the same thing, also not paying attention to the people around her. When we both realized that we were on a collision course to the same checkout register, it was too late for either of us to change direction as we were committed! We stood in line together for the most awkward minute of my life. I remember mumbling something, and I hope it wasn't, "How have you been?"!

Another time, I took over an office and retail portfolio in Wichita, Kansas, and one of the assets we owned was a fairly large shopping center where a women's lingerie store was one of the tenants – think Victoria's Secret knockoff. Our security staff was in-house, which is rarely a good idea as I have always viewed engaging a third-party security company as similar to an insurance policy. If there is an incident where we get sued, I am bringing in our security company to indemnify me per the contract.

I was in the process of separating the officers who were keepers and the ones who were not and telling the third-party company I was looking to hire who to hire and who not to. One incident made that decision quite easy for me as it related to a particular security officer.

The owner of the women's lingerie store called shortly after I was assigned the portfolio and told me that one of my officers would come into the store quite often and just hang around and stare at the merchandise, sales ladies and customers, and this was not the first time she has reported this to property management. I told her I would take care of it.

This particular security officer was a big dude. His brother was a linebacker in the NFL! The first thing I did was call the Wichita police department and told them that I was going to fire an employee who might become belligerent, and I would like one of their officers to be in the lobby of the management office when this event occurred. My recollection is they agreed, but at the last minute, the officer got called away for an emergency and never showed up. I had the property manager and another security officer sit in with me, and thankfully, the firing occurred without incident.

Another time, I had a property manager in Orlando who was using her company Home Depot card to purchase items for her home, including a pressure washer and items for her child's teacher and classroom. Not only was she a crook, but I came to find out that so was my predecessor, who she reported to and was having an affair with. I determined that my predecessor was creating unneeded capital projects and getting kickbacks from the contractors. It gets worse, or juicier as this was like a car wreck that I couldn't look away from as I rode past. I was speaking with the chief engineer to see if he knew anything about these events and, as we were walking past a small potted tree that was at the entrance to an alcove under an indoor staircase in one of the two-story buildings in the office park, I noticed a used prophylactic hanging off one of the branches. There is a Christmas ornament joke in here somewhere, but I am not going to make it! Since this was something I didn't see every day, I pointed it out to him. He told me that the day maid was known to do sexual favors for tenants in exchange for cash. Talk about an amenity! I asked the chief if he thought this was acceptable behavior, and he said he did not. I changed out day maids and gave the janitorial company 30 days' notice the next day.

I told the property manager to stay away from the office for a few days until I got things "sorted out." When I finally had my evidence, I set a meeting with her for 9:00 AM the next morning. I wanted someone else in the room with me (which is always a good idea) as the company I was working for didn't really have a human resources person, so I called our security company and told the account representative that I wanted the most intimidating looking woman they had to meet me at 8:30 AM. They did not disappoint. The security officer they sent was about 6'2" and probably 300 lbs of mostly muscle. We shot the breeze for a while, and she told me she used to be in the Ironworkers Union in Chicago and could bench press 315 pounds. I had no reason to doubt her. I set her up in a chair in the back of the room and told her she didn't have to say anything, just sit there. The property manager was right on time and took one of the guest chairs on the other side of my desk. When I told her that this was her last day with the company, she started getting loud stating that she was going to sue the company and me personally, etc. It was at this point that the security officer cleared her throat, and the property manager turned around to see who was there. Let's just say that the rest of the termination meeting went off without a hitch and I never heard from this person again.

There was an interesting follow up to this Orlando property manager termination. That week, I did a thorough tour of the office park and was stopped in my tracks when I walked into a larger tenant improvement project that was in progress. I was tipped off that there may be a problem when the CEO of the tenant called me to complain about shoddy workmanship and the project not being completed on time. When I walked the project, I noticed that the drywall was installed in a non-workman-like manner and there was no superintendent-like person around that I could talk to. I got the contact information of the 'general contractor' from my chief engineer and set up a meeting with her the next day. When we met, besides questions about shoddy workmanship, I had an invoice for about $90,000 that was obviously inflated. She arrived with her 30-year-old son, who she told me was the superintendent. We walked the space, and to say it was embarrassing would be an understatement. We went back to the management office (which was now my office as I was now the de facto property manager), and I went down the line itemized invoice, and after discussing each item, I told her that what work wasn't fabricated on the invoice was done so poorly that I would have to bring in a real general contractor to rip out all the drywall and essentially start over. I told her that all I was going to pay was a couple of hundred dollars for her dumpster fees.

It was at that point that her son, a 30-year-old man, mind you, started crying like a baby into his mother's shoulder. The contractor/mom shot me a mean look while patting her son's back and said to me something like, "See what you have done? You have upset him." I told her that this was her doing and asked if she actually had a Florida general contractor's license. She admitted that she did not and was actually an interior designer who was a friend of the former property manager. By this time, the son was a sweaty mess with a face full of mucous, which made me feel very uncomfortable. I really wanted to just get up and leave, but it was my office. I asked them to leave, and they eventually did and I never heard from them again.

My approach to terminating one's employment is as follows.

1. Always have someone else physically in the room with you in the off chance the person getting fired accuses you of anything and you need a witness.

2. Have the severance package (if there is one) with you to hand to the person and explain it needs to be returned in X days or it will expire.

3. Have a checklist of items the employee needs to return with you.

4. I never make small talk and get right to the point. I typically lead off by saying, "This will be your last day with XYZ company. We will need to collect your cell phone, computer, access card, etc., before you leave". I give them the severance package and adjourn our meeting. I have found that keeping this termination meeting short and sweet is by far the best approach.

5. If the person wants reasons for their dismissal, I will either tell them in a concise manner or simply say that we feel it is in the best interest of the company. This entire script should be discussed with the senior human resources person prior to the termination meeting.

6. Unless the actions leading up to the dismissal are unconscionable, I like to give one written warning before terminating one's employment.

Chapter 14

Interesting Responses to Job Postings and Random Funny Lines

When we posted an ad for an assistant property manager at Colonial Properties Trust, we received resumes from people who apparently thought their prior work experience made them viable candidates.

1. Waitress at Cracker Barrel

2. Lifeguard

3. Rocket scientist at NASA whose prior annual salary was $450,000

One person who didn't show up for an interview called to reschedule after the fact and his excuse for not showing up was that he remembered his daughter's wedding was that day.

Another guy who simply didn't show up called to reschedule after the fact, and his excuse was that he had to move the day of the interview.

Your daughter getting married and moving are two fairly large life events and I would think these people would have at least put them on their calendars!

My Wichita property manager thought I was a little high-strung and offered to take me for a ride in an open-cockpit crop duster plane. I thanked him and politely declined.

When I was a property manager with Advantis, I was driving to lunch with the asset manager, who was in town from Connecticut, when we barely avoided an accident. He told me that if I killed the asset manager, they would just send a new one. I thought that was a pretty funny line.

I had a janitorial company offer me a week-long vacation to a resort in Mexico in return for giving them the contract. I told him I didn't like tacos.

I had some class C strip centers in South Florida, Birmingham and rural Georgia. You know, the type with no real anchor to speak of with a nail salon, barber, mom-and-pop grocery, questionable insurance broker, etc. If a tenant didn't pay the rent, the owner would put glue in the front and rear door locks and insert a toothpick in the keyhole with a note that said simply, "Pay your rent."

Another "trick" this owner had was to put a junked car as close as possible to the front door at night to greet the tenant in the morning as a gentle reminder to pay their rent.

Chapter 15

Management and Leadership Principles I Have Come to Live By, or You Can't Make This S**t Up!

Managing and leading people is not an inherent skill. It is learned and cultivated through trial and error over many years. Whatever recent success I have had working with my staff was developed over several decades and I didn't consider myself even a competent manager and leader of people until I was in my forties. Here are some of the concepts I have adopted over the years.

(Almost) never reprimand an employee in front of other employees. Showboating makes you look bad to observers and embarrasses the person you are speaking with. This person will immediately lose respect for you, which will be difficult to regain. Respect is a goal that must be earned and this is not the way to do it. Rather, take the person aside and clearly state the issue you have with their performance or behavior. If and when they start giving you excuses, consider them, but don't back down unless they bring forth information you haven't previously known about or considered. If and when they get off topic, stay the course and firmly bring them back on topic. Always try to end these one-on-one meetings on a positive note by showing the individual that you are trying to help them and have their best interests at heart, which you should.

I have been accused of "coddling" some of the people who reported to me, but I disagree with this assessment. I have always looked at my department as a "family" and have tried to keep issues within the family whenever possible.

Guys who move furniture and 20-year veteran senior property managers of Class A multi-tenant office buildings are very different people, but the management and leadership principles that I have found to work the best are quite similar.

Most people are somewhat hesitant to tell co-workers that they don't know something. I have had building engineers tell me, my property manager or my regional chief engineer that they know how to repair a heat pump when all they really know how to do is to remove the existing unit that doesn't work and replace it with a new unit. There is nothing wrong with not knowing how to do something, but there is everything wrong with saying that you do when it is simply not true. In the heat pump example where the maintenance engineer told the regional chief that he could repair the heat pump but really couldn't, the situation went from bad to worse quickly. A week later, the regional chief asked the maintenance engineer why it wasn't repaired, and the maintenance engineer knew he was stuck. Instead of simply telling the truth by saying he was embarrassed to say he didn't know how to repair a heat pump, so he said he did and was sorry, which still would have been OK, he made up another story about being too busy. This prompted the regional chief to ask why he didn't let him know this so other arrangements could be made, and by the time this issue crossed my desk, way too much time had been wasted, and there was distrust in the maintenance engineer by his boss, the regional chief. The entire incident could have been avoided if the maintenance engineer simply admitted he didn't know how to repair the darn heat pump in the first place.

Telling the truth is a novel concept. When I was in my early '20s and owned the moving and storage business in New York, Brewer & Son, I joined the local Teamsters Union as I found out several times the hard way that a moving company had to be in the union in order to work in many office buildings in New York City. Luckily (kind of), I had a good "Rabbi" and met a few people who gave me advice, one of which was Roy Barnabie with Tishman Speyer. Roy told me to stay as close to the truth as you possibly can and not to trust my mother, which was another way of saying not to trust anyone. I made the former part of my DNA but decided to modify the latter piece of advice to the Ronald Regan line of "Trust but verify."

Back to management and leadership. Telling the truth works both ways. Not only should an employee tell his or her boss when he or she lacks the skill set to perform a particular task, a boss should be honest with his or her employees about his or her own shortcomings. Admitting to not knowing something or that you (the boss in this case) lack a particular skill is not a sign of weakness. Rather, it is a sign of intelligence and leadership. Let me explain. If I tell someone who reports to me that I need his or her help because they are much better at figuring out accruals than me or that I don't know squat about electric boilers, I gain their trust because they know I am being honest with them. I wouldn't say I know nothing about electric boilers if I actually do! Gaining trust is a foundational piece of being a leader and gets people to believe in you and follow you. It also shows that humility is part of my character, which is an endearing quality. It shows that I have a smaller ego, and I am confident enough in myself to admit when I don't know something, which are all leadership skills. People tend to respect people who tell the truth and are like them in some ways. Stay as close to the truth as you possibly can. Thanks, Roy!

My first day at the Wilson Company, one of the administrative assistants approached me, introduced herself and told me that everyone was chipping in for Roberta's (not her real name) abortion. She then asked me how much I was going to contribute. Besides considering what an unusual request this was, to say nothing about the inappropriateness of it, I also needed to come up with an answer. At the time, I was not savvy enough to think to say, "Let me get back to you," as this is usually a good stalling tactic in any situation, both in business and in life. Per the paragraphs above, when asked a question you truly don't know the answer to, saying that you don't know but will find out and get back to them is almost always acceptable. That answer obviously wouldn't apply in this case, however!

I felt pressured to answer the question timely, especially with the first day (and first ever real estate job) jitters having kicked in. My first thought was the easy answer, and the one I rationalized would be best to help me "fit in." I was close to saying something like,

"How about $20 (this was 1995, after all), but I then immediately pivoted to being deemed a patsy as I had no idea if this request was legit or not. Instead, I told her that I didn't get Roberta pregnant and if I did, I would pay for the entire abortion myself.

In no way, shape or form do I want this book to turn political, nor am I giving away my position on abortion. I said what I said to take a strong stand and show that I was a person of substance who wouldn't always go along with the crowd. This lady turned on her heels and walked away, knowing that I wasn't afraid to voice my opinion, no matter how unpopular. I was never asked to contribute to anything again during my time with Wilson, except for the United Way, which I happily did.

Another interesting person at The Wilson Company was my engineer. He was experienced, and I knew nothing, and he was fond of reminding me of this fact. He also thought a lot of himself, including being a ladies' man and a workout warrior, even though I could never understand why on either front. One day, I noticed there was a pull-up bar installed in a storage room. When I asked him about it, he said it was his and asked me if I wanted to bet $20 that he could do more pull-ups than me. I was pretty sure I could double his number in this endeavor, but I didn't want to take his money and drive the wedge that existed between us deeper than it already was. I told him that I didn't want to bet but was open to a friendly competition. He went first and did eight or nine pullups. I went next and did 10 pullups and stopped even though I had more in the tank. I wanted to beat him but not embarrass him. He then asked me if I wanted to race him in a foot race on the road that leads to the loading dock. I knew I could easily beat him in a foot race and also knew that the race would draw a crowd. If I let up and only beat him by a little, it would be obvious that I was taking it easy in him, which would have embarrassed him even more than simply losing. Instead, I offered to run backwards while he ran forwards. He was hesitant because if I beat him running backwards, he would really look bad, and if he won, it wouldn't mean as much because, well, I was running backwards. He agreed to the race under these parameters because he just couldn't help himself. I wore loose-fitting pants the day of the race and brought my sneakers. There were probably 20 spectators made up of vendors and tenants. The race was probably about 40 yards, and he beat me by a few steps, which was perfect. He saved face, a few people applauded and I believe the event brought us closer together. He was still a horse's ass, but maybe not so much of one as he had been.

When I left Delma Properties and joined IPC in 2005, I was given, among other assets, asset management responsibility for a nearly one million square foot multi-tenant office building in downtown Dallas. The address when I started this assignment was 2121 San Jacinto, but we changed it to 2100 Ross to give it some gravitas, as Ross Ave is the main street that runs through the arts district of the Dallas central business district. Trammell Crow managed and leased the building for us, and they essentially "ran" Dallas from a commercial real estate perspective, as their corporate headquarters was in Dallas. Trammel Crow Center was across the street with its large statues and outdoor artwork scattered over the lawn, which added to the mystique and aura of Crow, as they were called in abbreviated form. In short, they reminded me of the Mafia, from what I have read in the newspapers growing up and living in NY in the '70s and '80s, not necessarily by their actions but more by how people at other companies feared them as it was evident that they were held in some kind of weird high esteem.

Before I go on, let me say that I truly enjoyed my time in Dallas, and I found it interesting that the people (I am making a huge generalization here) gave the impression that they were pretty damn special and the other 49 states were lucky to have Texas as a member. After being ingratiated into the Dallas commercial real estate community, I will tell you that the people I met were extremely sophisticated in getting deals done and solving problems. Our partner in the 2100 Ross deal was The PNL Companies, who was also a tenant, and I could not have asked for a better group of people to partner with, especially Dan Levitan, who may be the only Eagles fan living in Dallas!

Anyway, back to the story and my point. When I started with IPC, we were choosing an architect to design the main lobby (actually two main lobbies if you know the building) we were going to renovate, as well as the four or five below-ground garage elevator vestibules. The total cost of the project was approximately seven million dollars, if I recall correctly. Crow assumed they would manage the project and I was informed their construction management fee was 5%, which penciled out to a healthy $350K CM fee. This was not my first rodeo, although this was the largest project I had been involved with up to that point, and 5% seemed at the high end of the market range to me.

Although Crow had the management and leasing assignments for the asset, I was not contractually obligated to give them the construction management for this or any project, so I decided to bid it out. I received two or three proposals, and the lowest bid I received was for 3.5%, which was a savings of $105K over what Crow was charging me. To put it another way, $105K was likely close to my base salary in 2005 and saving my employer my salary made me feel like I was worth the investment they made in hiring me. Let me also say here that choosing the low bidder is not always the best route to take for multiple reasons, not the least of which is the old adage, "You get what you pay for."

I vetted the low bidder by calling references and speaking with our architect, Andre Staffelbach, who was one of the most interesting men I have ever met. His passion outside the office was cycling, and he and I spent a fair amount of time discussing this sport as I was doing triathlons at the time. This was also when Lance Armstrong's Tour De France victories was captivating many people in the country and around the world, and Lance was born and raised in Dallas. I regret never riding with him (Andre, not Lance), although there would be some embarrassment on my part as he would constantly have to slow down to allow me to catch up. He was probably 20 years older than me!

As an aside, this renovation project won an award and made the prestigious Corporate Interiors No. 8 book published in 2007. This project can be found on pages 209-216 of that publication.

The construction management company that was willing to manage my project for 3.5% or approximately $245K checked out on all fronts, so I spoke with Gary Gillis (not real name), who ran operations at Crow when we ran into each other at a function and asked him to lower his construction management fee percentage. He said he couldn't do this as they charge 5%, and that was that. I thanked him for his interest in managing my project and informed him that I would be using the services of another firm due to cost. His initial reaction was a look of confusion, but then it turned to anger. He muttered something like, "I understand," and walked away. I knew this wasn't the last I would hear on this issue and I was right.

Gary immediately elevated the issue to his boss, Bruno Lemon (not his real name), who called my boss, Lis Wigmore, the COO of IPC US REIT. Lis is a terrific person, a savvy business woman and someone I respect a great deal. She called me, told me she got a call from Bruno and asked to hear my side of the story. I told her there was only one side and we were not obligated to use Crow for construction management services and I was simply trying to get the best bang for our buck for quality work. She agreed that my course of action was correct, called Bruno back and told him that, all things being equal, we want to use Crow for construction management services. Crow dropped their fee to 3.5% and we completed the project on budget and on time.

This is another example of standing up for what you believe. It is easy to fall in line with everyone else, but standing your ground on an issue you feel strongly about will set you apart from the pack. This is an example of where I truthfully was about to pinch hit for Mickey Mantle – see chapter 18 for my favorite quotes.

Leaders must be arrogant enough to believe they are worth following and humble enough to know that others may have a better sense of the direction they should take. They must believe in themselves but be willing to put the organization's needs above their own.

To the managers reading this, think big picture more often and don't be afraid to ask questions and challenge the status quo when you think you have a better way of doing things.

To the non-managers, you don't have to be a manager to be a leader in the way you conduct yourself and truly care about the organization you work for.

Chapter 16
Interviewing

I have interviewed literally over 200 people in the last two-plus years of my work career, mostly because of company growth and, to a lesser degree, due to turnover. I have had six interviews on a Saturday because I simply couldn't fit them in during the week.

The first question I ask a candidate on the interview is if he or she went on our website. If they say no, the interview is over, with few exceptions. I tell them that I have prepared for the interview by Googling the companies they have worked for so I would know as much about them as possible, and it defies logic that I am more interested in the interview, in their future for that matter, than they are. I already have a job with a company I want to retire from, yet I took the time to prepare, and they didn't!? I calmly tell them that the interview is over and explain why. I sometimes get apologies; sometimes they feel insulted, and sometimes I just get blank stares.

When I ask the website question, I know the answer before they open their mouth to speak, just by the look on their face. If the look is a confident smile, I know they went on the website. If the look is deer in headlights, I can see the wheels turning with the candidate asking him or herself, "What can I say to make this question go away so we can proceed with the interview?". It gets embarrassing for the candidate and for everyone else from my company in the room with me when their answer is that they did go on our website, and I start asking probing questions about our company, and they don't have the answers. Sometimes, they cop to their untruth, but more often than not, they either continue to expand on their fabrication or say something like, "Well, I just skimmed over the website."

When they say they haven't been on our website and I ask them why not, the worst answer is that they did not have enough time or they were busy. I will typically respond by saying that I had enough time to read every word of their resume and research their former or current company, and I am also busy, to the tune of 70-hour work weeks.

Let me say at this juncture that I realize that I may sound like a horse's ass, but this is not my intention. My intention is to educate the candidates for their next interview and not to waste my time or the candidate's time when there is now zero chance they will be considered for the position they had come for.

Besides the usual questions as to why the candidate left their past jobs and why they are considering leaving their current one, I like to probe into their personal life a bit as I need to know who this person is as it relates to personality, motivation, integrity, ambition and grit. I want to know what their parents did for a living and, who their mentors were along the way, and why.

Here are some probing and out-of-the-box interview questions that can give valuable insight as to who the candidate really is. Please feel free to use them as you see fit.

1) Tell me about a time when you thought about giving up but didn't, and tell me what you did instead.

2) Have you ever worn a costume at a Halloween Party?

3) Tell me something that is true that almost no one argues with you on.

4) Characteristic that your closest friends love and hate about you.

5) A hammer and nail cost $1.10 together. The hammer costs $1.00 more than the nail. How much does the nail cost?

6) If I spoke to a varied group of people who have known you throughout your life, what 3 adjectives would they all agree to describe you?

7) If we are sitting here in 12 months reminiscing about a great year we are having, what did we achieve together?

8) What one person influenced your leadership style and how?

9) What motivates you to get out of bed in the morning?

10) What was the last event in your life that didn't work out, and what did you do afterwards?

11) What is not on your resume' that you want to tell me about yourself?

Chapter 17
Email Writing Tips

Some things to keep in mind when writing emails to tenants:

1. People generally don't want to read emails so keep it short.

2. Make sure all pertinent facts are included and all non-pertinent info is excluded.

3. The goal is for your reader to not have any questions after reading your email.

4. Reread every email you write before hitting 'Send.'

5. Don't put an email address into the 'To' line until you are absolutely ready to hit 'Send' and make sure you are sending the email to the intended person.

6. You don't get another chance at this. Once you hit "send," you likely can't take it back.

If there is one thing you take with you after reading this book, make it #4 above. It typically takes between 5 and 10 seconds to reread the email you just wrote, depending on its length, and it is well worth every second. The spell check function doesn't capture words that you didn't intend to use, and most importantly, it doesn't capture the tone you didn't intend to convey.

I know you have 17 other things to do, and you just don't have the time or patience to reread the email that you are about to hit 'send' to, but stop, take a breath and remember that the most important tenant in your portfolio is the one you are emailing to now (Chapter 12, Core Belief #12). Don't give them an opportunity to get a poor impression of you by sending an email that doesn't flow smoothly, contains grammatical errors or, worse yet, sends a tone you didn't intend. When I send an email that is particularly pointed or strong, I will often take a walk around the building inspecting something, giving myself one last chance to make sure I really want to send the message in such an aggressive fashion.

Chapter 18
Leverage in Negotiating

When negotiating, the most important thing to know before you start is who has the most leverage and who needs the win more. Sometimes, one person has the leverage up to a point, but beyond that point, the leverage shifts to the other person.

When I was with Morning Calm Management, we acquired a 900,000 sf multi-tenant office asset in Dallas where the incumbent property manager decided to remain with the seller. I needed to hire a property manager and, in a perfect world, a senior property manager, as this was a big asset for us. I interviewed perhaps a half dozen people and I liked a young lady who was an assistant property manager with about four years' total commercial real estate experience. I could have taken the easy way out and hired one of the 20+ year vets that I met, but the risk here is that they are too set in their ways to embrace how we looked at the commercial real estate world. Also, I get a great deal of satisfaction in seeing a young person's career path trend upward over the years, knowing that I may have played a small role in their advancement and success. If given the choice with a department of, say, 15 property managers and assistant property managers, I would have three of them with over 20 years of experience and the remaining 12 with less than five years under their belts. This way, I would have some help in training and mentoring the less experienced people, with the majority eager to learn and be mentored. I would be remiss if I didn't also admit that first time and/or younger property managers can be had for a lesser salary, thereby helping the asset's NOI and associated value.

This particular candidate was in her mid-20s and was making $75,000 annually with a national third-party real estate company and, as stated in the preceding paragraph, was an assistant property manager with about four years' experience. I offered her an annual salary of $85,000, complete with all our benefits and year-end bonus potential. She verbally accepted, although I could tell the wheels were turning as I heard some hesitation in her voice. I told her to sleep on it for a night and to call me the next day with her final decision. She asked me if the offer was negotiable, and I told her that everything is negotiable if one has leverage.

She called me the next day and said she was worth $95,000. When I asked her why she thought this, she stated that she had almost five years of experience, she helped manage a large portfolio for an institutional owner and the amount of work and responsibility would be more than she currently had. I responded by telling her that all that was true, but I would not be increasing my original offer. She seemed confused and reminded me that I said my offer was negotiable. I corrected her by reiterating my statement from the previous day that everything was negotiable IF one had leverage, and she didn't have any. I reminded her that she was an assistant property manager for a relatively short amount of time who never had to make any tough decisions and essentially simply did what she was told. I explained that it was I who was taking all the risk in this instance as this was our first foray into the Dallas market, and if we fell on our face either on the leasing or management front, it would be a huge blemish on our record, not only to our investors but also to one of the most sophisticated commercial real estate markets in the country. If she failed, she was young and had plenty of time to recover and could always spin her time at Morning Calm favorably on subsequent interviews. I also reminded her of the fabulous opportunity this was for her and the fact that we would have a detailed curriculum for her and almost unlimited support not only from me but from our director of property management and our accounting team, not to mention an engineering staff, led by a chief engineer who was at the top of his game.

I suggested that we both sleep on it and we would chat the next day. She called first thing in the morning and asked me to send an offer letter for her to sign. I thanked her for her interest and told her I was reneging on the offer and I would keep looking. She was angry and confused when I told her that the reasons she gave for wanting more money were weak and showed her immaturity. I suggested she use this as a learning experience, ask for more responsibility at her current job and come back stronger the next time she looks to change companies. The postscript here is that by waiting, I found an accomplished property manager who is an even better human being and has a tremendous future.

Back in about 2006, when I was at IPC, the former public REIT traded on the Canadian stock exchange, I had a building in downtown Baltimore located at 500 East Pratt Street. The building was a true class 'A' asset that was less than five years old and was located effectively on "Main and Main." It was about 300,000 square feet with larger, mostly Fortune 500 tenants on longer-term leases, essentially an asset manager's dream. The first floor had two spaces; one was vacant and the other was occupied by the Capital Grille, an extremely high-end restaurant chain, for those of you who aren't familiar. In addition to property management and construction, I also had leasing responsibility and was working with Lizanne Kelly (I believe that was her name) with Starbucks to put a store into the remaining first-floor vacancy. Lizanne and I had traded proposals back and forth, and I was wanting to close the deal. After several rounds of negotiations, I met with her in person on-site and told her that if we didn't get a deal done by the end of the week, I would stop negotiations and move on to the next tenant in line, even though there was none as I was bluffing.

My mistake was not realizing that I was negotiating with the 800-pound gorilla (Starbucks, not Lizanne), and I had little leverage as I needed Starbucks much more than they needed to be at my building. Lizanne thanked me and said she would be in touch before walking away. That was the last time I ever heard from her, as my phone calls went unreturned. The valuable lesson I learned was to negotiate from strength and use your leverage, or lack thereof, wisely.

Chapter 19
Some of My Favorite Quotes

"It's not the will to win, but the will to prepare to win that makes the difference."

Paul "Bear" Bryant, former head football coach at the University of Alabama

Just about everyone will say truthfully that they want to be a winner but few will put in the time and effort in preparation that it takes to actually come out on top.

"This ain't no party. This ain't no disco. This ain't no fooling around."

David Byrne, lead singer of The Talking Heads, Life During Wartime

Life is not a dress rehearsal. I am as guilty as the next guy in forgetting this sometimes.

"A person doesn't really become whole until they become part of something bigger than themselves."

Jim Valvano, former head basketball coach at the North Carolina State University

Jimmy V. was talking about a college men's basketball team, but he could have easily have been talking about a commercial real estate management and investment company.

"I came here to kick ass and chew bubblegum, and I am all out of bubblegum."

-Rowdy Roddy Piper, former professional wrestler

I love professional wrestling. Please don't judge me!

"Don't have $100 shoes and a $10 cent squat."

-Louie Simmons, deceased owner of Westside Barbell, arguably the most famous powerlifting gym in the country

It is performance and effort that counts, and nothing else.

"The question isn't who is going to let me; it is who is going to stop me."

-Ayn Rand, Russian-American author

"The man who moves a mountain begins by carrying away small stones."

-Confucius, philosopher

"Flaming enthusiasm backed up by horse sense and persistence is the quality that most frequently makes for success."

-Dale Carnegie

"Most guys go to where the puck is. I go to where the puck is going to be."

-Wayne Gretzky, former National Hockey League player

"Strength is a choice. Weakness is an excuse."

-Not sure where I heard this

"You don't pinch hit for Mickey Mantle"

-Douglas Brewer, property management professional and regular guy

Sometimes, the safe and popular decision is the best decision. If Mickey strikes out, no one will point the finger at you. If you put Joe Palooka up to bat instead of Mickey and Joe strikes out, you look foolish and there will be finger pointing. There is a time and place for sticking your neck out, going against the grain and trusting your gut instinct.

"I never learned anything while I was talking."

-Larry King, former New York media personality

Many times, the best move is to shut up and listen.

"Never, never, never give up."

-Winston Churchill, former prime minister of England

"Give me six hours to chop down a tree, and I will spend the first four sharpening the axe."

-Abraham Lincoln, 16th president of the United States

Again, preparation is the key to success.

"Sometimes the cards ain't worth a damn if you don't lay 'em down."

-Jerry Garcia, lead singer of the Grateful Dead, Truckin'

Getting the ball to the two-yard line isn't enough. You need to score.

"The best are rarely the fastest, the strongest or the most technically skilled; often, they're just people unlucky enough to know real pain, which puts a race into context. At a certain distance, talent is superseded by the ability to just go on."

-Joseph Bien-Kahn, author of a Sports Illustrated article from the October 2022 edition about a paralyzed wheelchair racer named Ian Mackay.

I absolutely love this quote. To me, it means that grit and perseverance will oftentimes make you the winner, even if your opponent is more skilled than you.

"Life begins at the end of your comfort zones."

-Unknown

Try things that you have always wanted to do but didn't because you were afraid or hesitant. It is exhilarating and makes for a better life.

Chapter 20

Heroin to Hand Grenades or My Travels Through Yeehaw Junction

As a background to this chapter, it is important to understand that I have lived in the Tampa area since I moved to Florida from Long Island in 1992 with my wife and two young boys. Up until 2015, I had always had an office in the Tampa area, even though I was traveling for business most weeks. When Morning Calm Management sold Rivergate Tower (a 32-story round building and the tallest limestone building in the world, I am told) in downtown Tampa in August of 2015, I had a decision to make. I could either resign from my position with Morning Calm and look for a job-based in the Tampa area or move to the West Palm Beach area, where Morning Calm's corporate office was located at the time. I didn't want to leave Morning Calm as I saw a potentially tremendous future there for myself and for the company, and I would soon learn that these went hand-in-hand. I also didn't want to relocate my family from the Tampa area as my oldest son is handicapped and had some terrific friends, a job at Publix (a supermarket chain headquartered in Lakeland, FL I can't say enough good things about their hiring of handicapped individuals, not to mention the cleanliness of their stores and politeness of their employees) and a girlfriend (my oldest son, not me).

Instead of choosing one of these options, I invented a third option, which was to rent an apartment in Boynton Beach, equidistant between West Palm Beach and Boca Raton, from August 2015 to March 2020, when COVID hit. I would leave my house on Sunday afternoon, typically at halftime of Jets games during football season (yes, I am a lifelong Jets fan, so get your smirks and jokes out of the way now) to begin the four-hour drive and depart from the Morning Calm Management West Palm Beach (and later Boca Raton) office at lunchtime on Fridays, arriving back at my home in Tampa around 5:00 PM. I was typically home for 46 hours per week during this four-and-a-half-year period. This, of course, was when I wasn't flying to one of our out-of-state properties. After COVID, I continued to make the trip from Tampa to South Florida two or three times per month up until my retirement on March 8, 2024.

The halfway point of this trip from Tampa to West Palm Beach is Yeehaw Junction, a town in central Florida that sits at the intersection of State Road 60, U.S. 441 and the Florida Turnpike. It has been called Jackass Junction because of the mules that used to reside behind a local restaurant. It has also been called Junkie Junction because of the area's reputation as a secluded rendezvous for drug dealers. In its heyday, it was a flea stain on a map of Florida. Today, it consists of three gas stations, two of them being new. Oh yeah, there is the Desert Inn, which consists of two buildings – a bar and grille and a motel. The motel was closed when I started driving by in 2015, but the bar and grille was open and advertised the best frog legs in central Florida. I fought temptation and never stopped in. In 2019, a truck slammed into the Desert Inn, and its shambles remain today in the same state as it did that fateful day in 2019. I am not sure why the debris hasn't been cleared, but I am not surprised. In the 1930s, the Desert Inn was a brothel, and local ranchers rode there on burros, presumably for the frog legs.

I stop at one of the gas stations just about every trip to either use the restroom, get gas or grab an iced tea and see basically the same types of people – motorcycle club members, migrant workers and truck drivers. Naturally, I fit right in. If I didn't look like an off-duty police officer, I am pretty sure I could purchase just about whatever I wanted here if I hung around long enough.

About a mile west of Yeehaw Junction is a bar called the Y'all Come Back Saloon. This is another establishment I have successfully fought the urge to frequent. There is no point to this chapter other than me having stopped at the gas stations in Yeehaw Junction so often, I have come to actually like this quaint little town. Stockholm Syndrome comes to mind!

I didn't start traveling regularly for work until I was 41 years old and my two boys were in high school, so I was able to coach them in Little League, attend all parent/teacher conferences, chaperone class trips, etc. I am thankful that my employment up until this time didn't require any travel because I would have missed many of these special moments. A major takeaway from this book should be that family is more important than work. Sure, you will have to make sacrifices along the way, but don't miss the important family-related milestones and events, or you will regret it when you retire and reflect back on your career.

Chapter 21
Evaluating Proposals and Getting the Best Bang for Your Buck

I will venture to guess that when most property managers need a repair done that is less than $10,000, they get a proposal from their go-to vendor in that particular trade, skim over the proposal, sign it and send it back to the vendor. No fuss, no muss. This approach may be partially OK for, say, a chiller repair that is not covered under your preventive maintenance contract with Trane, for example, and you don't want to bring in another mechanical contractor for fear of future finger-pointing should a related issue arise three months from now, but I will never believe this approach is OK for, say, a series of curbing repairs around your building or some parking lot restriping or a larger plumbing repair.

In the case of the chiller repair, I totally get that you want to use the same mechanical contractor who has the preventative maintenance contract. This doesn't mean, however, that you don't question him on the cost. He already knows he is being awarded the job for the reason stated above, but does that mean you have to give him carte blanch on the cost without even trying to understand how he arrived at his number?

In the case of a larger plumbing repair, let's say you get a proposal for $9,850 from your favorite plumber. You know, the nice guy who you see at most BOMA or IREM lunches who takes you to lunch one or two times per year and pops into your office occasionally to say "hi." Before I go on, please understand that I have nothing against this guy. He is using the sales tactics that are available to him, and he is doing nothing wrong. If his crews do a good job with little or no issues, by all means, continue to enlist his services.

I understand that $9,850 is a relatively small amount compared to your two-million-dollar total operating expense budget, and if you capitalize this cost, it can easily be absorbed into any contingency line that may be in your capital budget, but I am here to strongly suggest that you don't think this way. If you can save $500 or $1,000 on every project like this that occurs over the course of the year, you may be able to move the needle even a little bit by year-end. After all, isn't this part of your job description? Don't you have a fiduciary responsibility to the owner and investors of your building? When you took the job to manage this thirty-million-dollar asset, wasn't it implied that you would think critically when performing all aspects of your job? Doesn't the buck stop with you when it comes to expenses and the budget?

I would ask my plumbing salesman friend and myself the following questions AFTER I bid the project to at least one other plumbing contractor.

1. What is the breakdown between labor and material?

2. How many man-hours do you have in this proposal?

3. Does the hourly rate per man pass the sanity check test?

4. Can we make this a not-to-exceed price based on the actual number of man-hours used?

5. Does the project really need to be done on overtime?

6. What exactly is that 'truck charge' for $150, and can we remove it?

7. "Look, man, I want to give you this job, but I have another bid for about the same amount. This project isn't budgeted, and, while not your problem, I need your absolute best price".

8. I would also Google the actual cost of the part to be replaced and see how large his markup is.

I know all this takes time, but I am here to tell you that it is worth the time. You are not in your position to make friends; your job is to manage the asset to the best of your ability. If you make friends along the way, great. If you don't, that is OK as well. Once vendors know that you will ALWAYS be questioning how they arrived at the amounts in their proposals, they will start including this information with each proposal. You want to develop the reputation that you are a manager who believes that a vendor deserves to make a fair profit but that you also want the very best price you can get for each and every job. Vendors need to earn your business and trust, and taking you to lunch and shooting the breeze at monthly meetings is fine, but their pencils need to be sharpened all the time when dealing with you.

When reviewing the vendor's proposal, it is critical to read every single word. This is easier said than done, as reading every single word takes commitment, dedication and, most of all, time when you have seventeen other things on your to-do list. Read every single word, anyway. I promise you will not regret it. Pay special attention to what IS NOT included. This Exclusions section can add to the cost and will often determine if you are comparing apples-to-apples when reviewing multiple proposals. It is rarely a good idea to sign a vendor's proposal as they have terms and conditions that will be advantageous to them only.

I will occasionally sign a vendor's proposal if I have an existing maintenance contract with them and there are no terms and conditions attached. When attaching a vendor's proposal as the exhibit to your one-time agreement or service agreement, remember to omit the vendor's terms and conditions and only include the cost and scope of work.

Chapter 22
Certificates of Insurance

We deal with certificates of insurance on a regular basis, but I would bet a week's salary (easy for me to say as I am retired with no income!) that 90% of the seasoned property managers out there would fail a simple quiz on this document. Just about all property managers are familiar with the sections of the standard Accord certificate of insurance but I don't think most really know what each section really means. I never understood why this document never got the attention it deserved with seminars or tutorials when we refer to it regularly and have portals on our property management software to keep them updated for both vendors and tenants. Many of us regularly accept them from our vendors and tenants without anywhere near a thorough understanding of what each section means or with only a cursory review before we file them. For the last thirteen years of my career, I had a terrific insurance broker, Brett Cutchin with Higgenbotham, who would annually put on a 90-minute seminar for my property management staff that was extremely informative and always got rave reviews. Thank you, Brett! Among the topics he covered were the following.

1. Can we 100% rely on the COI? The answer is a resounding 'No, but we do anyway.' COIs can be forged and can become void due to lack of payment. They are barely worth the paper they are printed on. Yes, I know the section on the lower right-

hand corner of the document titled 'Cancellation" states that the insurance company needs to give each certificate holder notice if the COI is canceled before the expiration date in accordance with policy provisions, but do we ever know what the policy says about this? No, we don't.

When I had my moving business, Brewer & Son, in New York in the 1980s, general liability coverage cost me $1500 per $1 Million of coverage. As I recall, many of the hi-rise office buildings in Manhattan required $5 Million of coverage, and $7,500 was a lot of money back then. Another regional mover I knew legitimately had $1 Million of general liability coverage but doctored the document to read $5 Million of coverage and would routinely turn in this false COI to meet the requirement.

2. If a tenant doesn't have any company vehicles, they don't need auto coverage, right? Wrong. What happens if a guest or invitee of the tenant hits someone in your parking garage or causes property damage with their personal vehicle and they don't have any or adequate coverage? The answer is the landlord may be brought into the lawsuit. If the tenant has auto coverage, this insurance can likely be applied towards the incident.

3. The state my building is located in says that a company with less than three employees isn't required to have workman's compensation coverage. This should be good enough for me,

right? Wrong. Many local moving companies technically have less than three employees, with the actual movers being third-party contractors. These people probably don't meet the criteria for a contractor, but they are listed as one anyway and receive 1099 forms at year-end instead of W2 forms. If a mover falls off the truck's liftgate and breaks his ankle, he will turn to his "employer" to pay for it. If the "employer" denies the responsibility, the injured mover will look to the landlord to pay. The landlord will then look to the tenant who hired the moving company, and it becomes an exercise in finger-pointing that could have been avoided if the landlord required all vendors who work in the building to have workman's comp coverage, regardless of what the state statute says.

4. If the COI says that my owner and the management company I work for are covered as an additional insured, I can rest assured I am covered, correct? Nope, in many cases, there needs to be a written contract stating that the vendor is required to name particular entities as additional insureds.

5. We all know that a waiver of subrogation means that the insurance carrier is prohibited from recovering money they paid on a claim, right?

6. We also know that, under the Commercial General Liability section, it is very preferable to have the General Aggregate Limit per Project and per Location boxes checked so coverage

will apply separately to each job. If only the per Policy box is checked, the possibility exists that there was a prior incident on another project that took most or all of the policy limit dollars.

7. We all know that a Fidelity Bond covers employee theft, right?

8. When is the landlord responsible for the tenant's property? The answer is never if the lease is written correctly.

I would be remiss if I omitted the fact that we didn't always follow Brett's recommended insurance requirements to the tee, as sometimes, as property managers, we have to make strategic and thoughtful business decisions. Yes, sometimes we have to pinch-hit for Mickey Mantle. For example, some of our properties were class C retail strip centers in areas of south Florida, Alabama and rural Georgia that, how shall I put this delicately, Starbucks will not be going into these markets anytime soon. If we had a prospective tenant who we thought would pay us rent on time every month but simply did not have Umbrella coverage and was not going to get it, I would waive this requirement in order to get the cash flow. We called this asymmetrical risk. Let's say I bid out my landscaping contract on a large office park, and the bids ranged from $16,000 per month down to $11,000 per month, for example, and I went ten feet deep in my due diligence on all three of the bidders, meaning I visited a few of their other accounts, called references, was comfortable that all three account managers had a 'servant's heart" and the scopes of work were identical. The $16,000 guy had shiny new trucks, and their technicians had on new uniforms, while the $11,000 guy had older equipment and uniforms. This would make sense to me as their pricing reflected this, but I couldn't care less as they were doing outside work, and it wouldn't impact my tenants. I also noticed that the $11,000 guy only had $1,000,000 of Umbrella coverage instead of the required $5,000,000 and had only $500,000 of Worker's Compensation coverage instead of the required $1,000,000.

Now I have a decision to make. Before I make it, I go to the $11,000 guy and tell him that I need him to raise his limits. He checks the cost with his broker and politely gets back to me, saying it is not worth the additional premium for the profit he would make off of my account. I respect his business decision, and I factor in paying the difference in premium myself, but I determine that inserting these additional dollars into the analysis brings them too close to the $16,000 guy. Now, the decision. Do I go with the $11,000 guy and add $750,000 of value to my asset (Savings of $5,000 per month = $60,000 per year at an 8% cap rate) while taking the liability risk or do I play it safe and do what most property managers would do and not take the chance? I think you know the answer. I would go with the $11,000 guy without hesitation to increase the value of my asset as long as I still got close to the same work product I would get from the $16,000 guy. Now, if this was an elevator contract, it would be a different story as poor elevator service will impact the tenant's desire to renew and give the building a negative reputation in the market place that competing brokers will use to their advantage. But does it really matter if the lawn gets cut 38 or 34 times per year? It doesn't matter to me if I can save five grand per month on operating expenses without the tenants being impacted!

Chapter 23
Year-End Annual Written Reviews

I have always looked forward to year end annual written reviews and put a great deal of time and effort into writing them. After all, this is a full year in a property manager's career we are discussing, and I have always thought that only two things should come before your career on the priority totem pole – family and religion (assuming you are a religious person). There were two rules I gave myself about these reviews that I never broke. One was to keep a file throughout the year on each person I was directly reviewing (not just sitting in on) and adding to it as the individual's actions throughout the year, good and bad, determined. The second was to ensure that there were never any surprises to the person I was reviewing in the December review. For example, if I noticed in March that the individual had a poor interaction with a tenant or vendor and I only told them about this in our December review, this was on me. It is critical that conversations like this take place timely regardless of how unpleasant they may be. I would not bring this poor interaction up in the December review since we had already discussed it in March. If I noticed improvement in this particular area, I would absolutely incorporate it into the review, however. If I thought that a property manager's variance report presentations needed some work and I only brought this up in December during the review, this would be a poor reflection on me and not the property manager. If I was that property manager, my first thought would be why Brewer sat through 10 or 11 financial meetings thinking my presentation needed work, and I am only hearing about it now.

In any review, multiple examples need to be included. Without examples, you are only speaking in generalities, which don't hammer your point home like specific examples do. The examples need to clearly and concisely make your point in a constructive manner, showing that you are trying to help the individual become a better professional version of themselves. Discussing areas of improvement needed are much more important than discussing areas of strength, but a boss can rarely win trust by only discussing weaknesses. Most people's egos (mine included) need to be stroked at least a little bit, and if a review only touches on areas that need improvement, which is another phrase for areas of weakness, the person being reviewed may feel like they are getting beaten down and backed into a corner and stop being engaged in the conversation. If, however, you sprinkle in positive, impressive things the person did throughout the year that created value, whether intellectual or monetary, they are much more likely to be receptive to what you say about the areas where they need improvement. This is starting to bleed into the psychoanalytical arena, and I would never suggest that I am anywhere near proficient in this area (just ask my wife), but I have found this to be true through experience.

I have found that the review is more effective if it is a conversation instead of me simply talking about the individual's strengths and weaknesses, what they did well and what the areas are where they need improvement.

Besides providing examples of actual events over the past year to back up your points made in the annual review, goals for the following year should be included. These goals should be measurable whenever possible, but many skills needed in the commercial property management business are simply not quantifiable. These include managing people, becoming a better leader, running projects, attaining a better understanding of how every dollar you spend impacts the value of the asset you are managing, etc. Other potential needed areas of improvement are quite measurable, such as making less mistakes in emails by rereading every one over a second time before you hit the 'send' button, drafting a budget, attending more BOMA and IREM monthly meetings, getting more involved in larger capital projects, etc.

To summarize, written year-end reviews should be constructive, contain examples, contain goals, be conversational and rarely contain surprises.

Chapter 24

My 15 Minutes of Fame

The New York Times

TUESDAY, AUGUST 14, 2012

THE NEW YORK TIMES BUSINESS TUESDAY, AUGUST 14, 2012

ITINERARIES

Convention Time, Clog Time

More Than Storms May Bedevil Summer Travelers

The Tampa Bay Times Forum in Tampa, Fla., where the Republican National Convention starts on Aug. 27.

By AMY ZIPKIN

Summer, with its often-violent storms, does not always play well with business travel. But the wildfires in the West and high-security events like the London Olympics and two political conventions are making this summer particularly challenging.

For those headed west, for example, the wildfires that forced hotel evacuations and closings in Colorado in June were the start of a record-setting fire season that is expected to continue into October and November. Last Thursday, the National Oceanic and Atmospheric Administration raised its prediction of hurricanes this season.

"We are increasing the likelihood of an above-normal season because storm-conducive wind patterns and warmer-than-normal sea surface temperatures are now in place in the Atlantic," said Gerry Bell, the lead hurricane forecaster at the Climate Prediction Center.

Then, of course, there are the man-made high-security events, beginning with the Summer Games, which ended on Sunday in London, and continuing with the Republican National Convention in Tampa, Fla., from Aug. 27 to 31, with an expected 50,000 visitors, and the Democratic National Convention for three days in Charlotte, N.C., starting on Labor Day, which is expected to attract 35,000 people.

Along with anticipated protests, the conventions may lead to road closings and general disruptions. What this all means to business travelers and employers, said Wendy Lane, a labor and employment attorney with Greenberg Glusker in Los Angeles who drafts travel policies for corporate clients, is "an extra level of delay as airlines maximize efficiency by canceling flights and consolidating flights."

To deal with the unexpected, business travelers may need self-reliance and flexibility. "The most important thing to pack is patience," said Henry Hartevelt, chief research officer and co-founder of the Atmosphere Research Group in San Francisco. He recommended that travelers explore alternative transportation options like trains and ferries. And he suggested carefully monitoring potential problems at their destination.

Exploring transportation alternatives made sense to Ray Berger, president and chief executive of MedjetAssist, a medical transport membership company in Birmingham, Ala. Mr. Berger said he was caught in a hailstorm at La Guardia Airport in New York in mid-July. Before

ham, he learned that the gate attendant was about to announce the cancellation of the flight. Mr. Berger hailed a cab to Penn Station, where he caught a train south to Baltimore. There, he was able to connect with another southbound plane with minutes to spare after persuading fellow passengers to let him cut in front of them at the security screening.

Weather, and other hazards, can now be better anticipated. Starting in late June, a system that sends emergency alerts via texts began operating on compatible cellphones. The system is the result of a partnership among the Federal Emergency Management Agency, the Federal Communications Commission and the wireless industry.

"This new public safety system allows customers who own an enabled mobile device in an area where their service provider has deployed the capability to

Douglas Brewer, a property management executive in Tampa, is urging office tenants to work from home.

receive geographically targeted textile messages alerting them of imminent threats to safety in their areas," said Damon Penn, FEMA program director. Events like tornadoes, hurricanes, an active shooter or an industrial accident will be the subject of notifications. Almost all wireless carriers have signed on, but consumers need to check if the service is available in their area.

As to the impact of the Olympics, Mark Naysmith, the Games readiness director at Deloitte UK, based in London, began in 2009 to consult with London-area clients about dealing with heightened security and transportation delays and traffic restrictions, all while anticipating a possible increase in business during the Olympics.

Some things did not quite work out as

and retailing, experienced rises in demand, according to a survey, the firm took during the first week of the Games, that balance was less than they had expected earlier in the year.

The end of the summer will bring the quadrennial nominating conventions. "Fair to say visitors are not going to be able to travel as freely as in a normal week in Charlotte and Tampa," said Daniel J. Kaniewski, deputy director of the Homeland Security Policy Institute at George Washington University.

Mr. Kaniewski said that in his experience, travelers should expect a range of issues, including, "fences, screening including metal detectors and rerouting transportation."

The possibility of such measures has given some Tampa businesses pause. Rhea F. Law, the chief executive and chairwoman at the law firm Fowler, White, Boggs, said she expected her office to start earlier, at 7:30 a.m., and close early while the convention was in town. Partners are being advised to work from home. The support staff will be paid their regular salary for shorter days.

Others are taking a more active approach. Douglas Brewer, an executive vice president at In-Rel, a property management firm that has its headquarters in Lake Worth, Fla., and offices in Tampa, said his firm sent an e-mail advising tenants of the city's Rivergate complex to stay away and work from home if possible. "I can see a half-hour commute turning into a two-hour commute," he said. He anticipates having to juggle to arrange building deliveries and garbage removal, and expects cleaning to be suspended until the building returns to a normal schedule.

In Charlotte, Michael Smith, the president and chief executive of the Charlotte Center City Partners, a nonprofit group that cultivates economic development in the central business district, where the convention will be held, is optimistic. He said he was encouraging the area's 83,000 employees to come to work despite tight security and expected transportation disruptions. The light rail line that serves the area will skip at least two stops and pedestrian access to streets and businesses near the Bank of America Stadium will be limited.

And Mr. Smith acknowledged that it would be difficult to find hotel rooms for anyone other than conventioneers. "There will be no room at the inn," he said. Sid Smith, executive director of the Charlotte Area Hotel Association, said business travelers might need to find

evice in an area where their service provider has deployed the capability to

BARBARA P. FERNANDEZ FOR THE NEW YORK TIMES

...uglas Brewer, a property management executive in Tampa, is urging ...ice tenants to work from home.

...eive geographically targeted textlike ...ssages alerting them of imminent ...ats to safety in their areas," said Da... Penn, FEMA program director. ...nts like tornadoes, hurricanes, an ac... shooter or an industrial accident will ...he subject of notifications. Almost all ...less carriers have signed on, but ...sumers need to check if the service is ...lable in their area.

...s to the impact of the Olympics, Mark ...smith, the Games readiness director

White, Boggs, said she expected her office to start earlier, at 7:30 a.m., and close early while the convention was in town. Partners are being advised to work from home. The support staff will be paid their regular salary for shorter days.

Others are taking a more active approach. Douglas Brewer, an executive vice president at In-Rel, a property management firm that has its headquarters in Lake Worth, Fla., and offices in Tampa, said his firm sent an e-mail advising tenants at the city's Rivergate complex to stay away and work from home if possible. "I can see a half-hour commute turning into a two-hour commute," he said. He anticipates having to juggle to arrange building deliveries and garbage removal, and expects cleaning to be suspended until the building returns to a normal schedule.

In Charlotte, Michael Smith, the president and chief executive of the Charlotte Center City Partners, a nonprofit group that cultivates economic development in the central business district, where the convention will be held, is optimistic. He said he was encouraging the area's 83,000 employees to come to work despite tight security and expected transportation disruptions. The light rail line that serves the area will skip at least two stops and pedestrian access to streets and businesses near the Bank of Amer-

Now may be a good time to familiarize yourself with Andy Warhol, who, in the late 1960's said, "In the future, everyone will be famous for 15 minutes."

In 2012, the Republican National Convention (RNC) was held in Tampa, Florida. Every major office building in downtown Tampa locked down for that week or literally had an eight-foot chain link fence installed around the building, except Rivergate Tower, you know, the 32-story round building, the beer can. (When In-Rel Properties acquired the asset in 2011, we tried to change the unofficial nickname to the champagne bottle, but it never caught on). Instead, during the RNC, we marketed the lobby of the four-story pavilion attached to the main building as an event venue and hired a professional event coordinator to handle the bookings. We received quite a lot of interest from the various political action committees (PACs) as well as groups like Politico and several private events and actually made a few extra dollars for us that week.

There were police officers from different cities in Florida on either foot, horseback, motorcycle or patrol car on almost every corner to fend off the crazies and potential acts of terrorism, and I am happy to say that the number of incidents were minimal. The City of Tampa, behind Mayor Bob Buckhorn, did a terrific job hosting the event, providing support and allowing the out-of-town security details to do their job.

A few weeks prior to the event, I sent a memo to the tenants advising them to allow their employees to work from home during RNC week, if possible, as a 30-minute commute could easily turn into a two-hour struggle. The memo also said that cleaning may be suspended or at least reduced, and deliveries may be impossible to predict. The theme of the memo was that the RNC was a once-in-a-lifetime event for downtown Tampa, and it was happening whether we wanted it to or not, and our work lives would, at the very least, be significantly inconvenienced for the week, and each tenant needed to take responsibility and make appropriate plans.

I reread and tweaked the memo more times than I can remember because it was likely the most important memo I was ever going to write. For this reason, I decided to write and send it myself instead of having my property manager do so. Little did I know that I had opened the proverbial "can of worms"!

Apparently, a tenant sent the memo to the Tampa Bay Business Journal who wanted to interview me for an article they were doing on the RNC, which was fine with me. The interview went off quite well, I thought, but as soon as the TBBJ was published, I started getting emails and phone calls from newspapers around the country wanting to interview me. I was interviewed by both the local Fox and CBS news channels, which also went well, although no one mistook me for George Clooney, a news anchor or even someone who was used to being interviewed.

The entire scene was getting a little bizarre as, up until this point, the only mammals who thought I was this important were my wife, my kids and my dog, and my dog was probably the only one who could never be convinced otherwise. When a guy called, who said he was from the New York Times, I didn't believe him but played along. He said he wanted to interview me over the phone and send a photographer to my Tampa office the following week to get a photo of me for the article that would appear on the front page of the Business Travel Section. I told him that the phone interview was fine, but I would be at our Lake Worth, FL, office on the day they wanted to send the photographer. He said that he would make the necessary arrangements and send a photographer up from Miami to meet with me at a time of my choosing.

I scheduled all meetings to be completed by 3:00 PM the day of the "photoshoot," even though I would have laid pretty heavy odds that no one would show. Much to my surprise, the photographer arrived a few minutes early and proceeded to pose me in various professional poses around the conference room while having my counterpart, who was down from Memphis, hold a spotlight at the angle the photographer instructed. 150 photographs (I am not exaggerating), and two hours later, we were done. If you think I ever let the Memphis guy forget that his job was to shine the spotlight on me, you are sadly mistaken. My seemingly endless (at least to him) stream of witty jokes included the suggestion that if this property management thing he was trying didn't work out, at least he now had another skill to fall back on!

As you can see from the accompanying photograph of the New York Times article, I achieved my 15 minutes of fame on August 14, 2012.

Chapter 25
Designations

You will notice three sets of letters after my name on the cover of this book. RPA stands for Real Property Administrator and is awarded by BOMA, Building Owners and Managers Association. CPM stands for Certified Property Manager and is awarded by IREM, Institute of Real Estate Management. CCIM stands for Certified Commercial Investment Member and is awarded by the CCIM Institute. The RPA and CPM are geared more for commercial property managers while the CCIM is less about building systems and more about financial analysis, although the concepts taught are critical to round out a property manager's knowledge base. I am quite proud of achieving these designations as I spent many hours attending classes and, studying for all three and taking final exams in the case of the CPM and CCIM.

If I had to do it over again, I wouldn't change a thing and would have invested the same amount of time and effort to attain these designations but, depending on how you market yourself, these letters and $6.05 will get you a venti chai tea latte at Starbucks. Here's what I mean.

When I got my RPA in 1998, I expected a larger-than-standard raise and, perhaps, a promotion. Didn't happen. Same expectations when I got my CPM in 2002, and again, that didn't happen. I came to realize that I was taking these classes and putting forth this tremendous effort for me and not necessarily for my company. I remember an asset manager telling me that he didn't think the building should have to pay for my classes as I should already have been trained before I started working with him. I couldn't really argue with him, so I didn't. With that said, I encourage every property manager reading this chapter to move heaven and earth to achieve one, two or all three of these designations if they are so inclined.

Yes, these designations will expand your knowledge base, making you more proficient at your job but the real value in having letters after your name in our industry appears when looking to change companies to advance your career. If I am looking to hire someone to report to me or someone to report to a manager who reports to me, having letters after their name on a resume could be what makes me offer them the position versus another candidate without letters. This has actually happened several times in my career. Knowing that a person has taken the time and put forth the effort to achieve one or more designations tells me that he or she is serious about his or her career and is motivated to get work done. These are attributes I want the people I work with to have. Having letters after your name is only a small part of my decision-making process when hiring someone, as their answers to my interview questions and their background make up the lion's share of whether I hire them or not, but if it is a jump ball, I will opt for the letters every time.

Chapter 26
Promotions

When I was in high school, I was the captain of the football and track teams. I was a pretty good player but that wasn't the reason why I was voted captain. I became the captain of both teams because I WANTED it, and I let everyone on the team know I wanted it, especially on the day of the vote.

The business world is no different. I have been promoted several times in my career, and on most of these occasions, it was because I let the right person know I wanted to get promoted. Often, people with the authority to promote don't realize that promoting you is a good idea, or even think of it, until you actually alert them to the fact that you are interested in advancing your career. Kind of like the "the squeaky wheel gets the grease" theory.

It should go without saying that you just don't burst into the senior person's office at your company out of the blue and announce that you want to get promoted and advance your career or send them an email with this fact spelled out in all capital letters. You will want to be somewhat subtle and work the fact that you are interested in taking on more responsibility if the opportunity ever presents itself into a conversation. Perhaps your company just expanded its management platform and the management of a hi-rise downtown office building may be up for grabs. Perhaps one of the property managers at your company is leaving for whatever reason, and the portfolio he or she manages is larger and more prestigious than the portfolio you are currently managing. Maybe your boss is getting promoted, and there is now a job opening at your company on the next rung of the ladder.

All of these scenarios are real and have happened in my career, and sometimes all it takes is for you to show the right person or people, in a respectful and subtle way, that you would like to be considered.

The author of the book touring a potential acquisition in West Palm Beach as part of due diligence. The author of the graffiti is unknown.

www.ingramcontent.com/pod-product-compliance
Lightning Source LLC
Chambersburg PA
CBHW041146110526
44590CB00027B/4138